Throwing Buns To Elephants

First a moment in memory of my father who went far too early :
I know I'm asleep, there's a silence that fills the air like the mist that floats around me. My viewpoint changes like cameras on a film set, sometimes high sometimes low. I wait challenging the mist, for the gap that I seek to appear, a re-occurring event. The shape appears a little camouflaged at first. A small slim figure, a child holding a ball under his arm. A football kit hangs from his body. Shirt aways over shorts, knobbly knees above dropping socks that rest on studded boots. An open face, round shiny blue eyes framed my strands of fair hair that dangle down from the pool of tangled mass above. A smile enters casting new cheek lines , radiating a warmth from the soft, tight skin. The eyes widen in innocence, nothing hidden there and I fall into them like an open book. I look up now, my father stands before me, tall, strong, solid. I know he's been there watching me from some shady hidden viewpoint. Always there my father, quiet, alone watching his son, proud I hope but never too sure, words, conversation not passing his lips too often. I hold the ball up

as he moves closer, my trophy, his trophy, our trophy. The knot that binds us in life, our union, our connection, the father and the son. He bends forward arms like iron as his hands grip my body. His force enters me as I rise into the sky, floating for a moment before settling into his cradled arm. I look back as we move away the mist clearing to reveal the top right angle of the goal post, my favourite target. A goal there again today as I see the ball, no longer in my hand once again strike the back netting. I float away safe, secure in my father's arms as the mist thickens behind us and the vision of the goal and ball disappears yet again. The memory remains still lodged deep in my mind, I will wait, I need to wait again for its return for I long to see my father again, even if its only in my dreams.

" Throwing Buns To Elephants "

I can feel it coming as the cool breeze curves around my ears, a small sweat drop forming as my pace steadies. My mind set on its target as my body glides over the ground, eating up the park. I drift past the trees, bushes and large areas of tall ferns that surround the sandy track dictating my route. I know the track well, my running ground, a testing task the circumference of Richmond Park. My long legs that carry me know their pace like moving through the gear box, smooth and controlled, trained and focused for the run. Life for me, leave my door, run to school, run to shops, run because that was me.

      The sweat drop grows in size and starts its journey, my skin sensitive to the breeze, notes its journey down my temple to the side of my eye. It is a lone drop, my pace and rhythm holding much in reserve. I don't sweat much, slim build on long bones, no unwanted kilos to shed, running a total enjoyment. The sweat drop now suspended held in place at the crease of my eye. Always a challenge to hold it there but my mind is not set, it starts to wander, something happened, something different that enters your mind, changes your focus, affects those chemicals that hold a straight line but what was it?

The school playground last week when everything stalled, time frozen, like films when they go into slow motion to capture the look, the feel, the intensity but actually now happening in real life. School break, for some reason I was goalkeeper, not my usual position I like scoring goals not saving them. I love football, I'm good at it, best in the school. I was leaning back against the wire netting, the two bent posts either side marking out the goal, Lonsdale Road behind me then the moving grey waters of the River Thames. My last year, nearly 16 years old, exams soon then football, every boy's dream, perhaps not but certainly mine. The ball far away down the other end, whistle soon, afternoon lessons ahead. Then it happened, across my line of sight she walked, four or five yards away, my eyes became locked on her like a radar target. Back straight, arms swinging purposefully, efficient lines, her face framed by short modern cut hair but only a sideways view. Her top tight around small breasts, long sleeves, tight, covering slim arms. Her skirt short, shapely legs in maroon tights entering weathered leather boots. A sharp memory that changed my life, I was held, a picture taken that's forever in my mind. Robby, our sports master passed her as she entered the school, I noted his backward glance, hard to avoid I thought along with the extra reddening of his face. Whistle in hand, five yards forward he blew, a little harder than usual I recall, its high pitched command signalling his control, ringing out its command, lunch break was over. Ex-army man, Robby, although sometimes I wonder if he knows about the ex bit. He controls things with a long stick, a sharp pointed end to emphasise his demands. We swarm like locusts to the wooden entrance door, my mind still distracted, lovely boots carrying my vision. A memory that changed my life. I was spellbound, invaded, a picture taken that's forever clear and defined in my mind.

The sweat drop sprung loose, escaped and rolled with certainty and purpose down my cheek. My pulse had increased, a loss of control, more sweat on my brow as I slowed to regroup. Ham Gate looms but that's enough for today, not the full picture, not the full park. I set a left turn and head off across to Pen Ponds. The control gone, a shorter route home, Sheen Gate, Palewell Park to Lower Richmond Road, school tomorrow, time needed I feel too regroup.

Things thrown in my bag I shut the front door to my bike padlocked below. An early ride to school along the river, I peddle harder than usual. There's a need in me, something I can't get a grip of, my usual controlled cruising speed not enough as the cold morning air chills my ears. The Thames full, high tide, a mass of water looking ominous and threatening as I pass so close to the high water line along Lonsdale Road. School kids starting to swarm, small groups starting to form. Bags strapped to their backs full of books and the relentless demand of more and more homework. I join the slow line to push my bike across the playground to the bike shed behind the school. I find myself looking around, my head high, searching, wanting to see again, wanting things to slow, wanting the experience again, definitely to see her, to be held.

      The assembly bears no fruit, the morning ritual before lessons. Barnes Boys, my school, our school, old style, small, only 150 assorted boys. I say assorted as that's what we are, not only tall, short, chubby , thin, but a mixed bag in nationality. Two Thai boys recently arrived whose names were quickly vandalised to Sooty and Cherry. They specialised in Kung Fu and went straight into the school football team as defenders. Their contribution is the main reason we are pushing to win the local school's league this season much to the dislike of the so called grander schools in the area. The teachers line the sides of the assembly outside their respective rooms. Their influence, knowledge, to be passed on to any receptive boy. Their techniques for gaining your attention all different, all knowledgeable in their own topics. Good teachers finding their way for various reasons to this small school along Lonsdale Road.

    I pay them more attention, my height a clear advantage. Spencer my English master, I like him a lot, tough on the spelling, my weak point. Always twenty times this, twenty times that. He has his ways, calling you up to stand next to him as he sits checking your weekend efforts to make multiple words into interesting stories. His hand has a way of gripping your inner thigh acting to pull you closer. Noting your reaction, leaning in, leaning out, I lean out. He earns your respect, I try hard with my stories but the spelling escapes me. He gives me a well done as I look down over his thinning head at the spidery red ink markings below.

    Elliott, Max Elliott our maths teacher, short and heavy set. He fidgets side to side always wanting to get on with things. His room behind, waiting to absorb his clan. Modern maths, now a new thing in the classroom but it leaves me confused. I'm good at sums, numbers I understand but when you get to the end of the alphabet, what do XY and Z add up to?

Mr Stroud our deputy head, always shining shoes to add importance to the impressive lines on his dark suit trousers. His slim build, straight back, silvery hair, smart uniform, everyday, set, set. Respected, polished in his deliveries, makes you interested in science. Time passes quickly in his classroom, there is always amusement in his featured topics. The pages of the reproductive organs of the rabbits have all been glued together in his books, obviously not an area for young minds to venture for examination or question in his class!

A couple of new teachers Geoff Morris and Tom Madison bringing their fresh input of enthusiasm and knowledge to pass on to any open, receptive mind. Always new faces to fill in the gaps but never able to replace the established hierarchy. Not a school to fulfil young, career minded teachers but solid for those that are looking for a comfort zone. A short visit get the school year over and look elsewhere for a future, a challenge, a career.

We file out into our rooms, weekly routines, Monday here, Tuesday there, Education? Older now, getting nearer the end, fodder for the work force although they don't teach us that. A new wave of energy, new times, something in the air, youth sweeping out the old, pop music, flower power, freedom from the old rules. Where will it end ? California? San Francisco? or possibly just lining up at the local dole queue.

Morning classes over, I'm back in goal looking. The game goes on around me, my disinterest unusual as I stand waiting. I play the part but a soft goal goes in. I study the passing cars, note the drivers, a few pull in at the girls school next door. Who was she? Will I ever see her again?

The afternoon sets me back in gear, games lesson, my favourite. Robby at his best, his self designed obstacle course set out in the school hall. Great, back in the army days as I note the smile that crosses his red blotchy face. Over this, under that, ten push ups here, ten star jumps there, hanging ropes to jump and swing. Robby's face reddens more as the afternoon progresses. His magic stick, the sharp end especially forcing more from the heavy set lads. Enjoying his power, position of authority, the hall hums with spent energy.

The bell rings and the hall is flooded with fleeing students in disarray. A rush only to escape the confines of the walls, outside they chat, walk slowly, linger in groups, school finished for another day. I sit on my bike chatting to friends, arranging a meet up later a kick about at the back of the flats. The school band starts up, rehearsals, an hour consumed. I know the routine well, cymbals, tambourine player a couple of years back, eager to please then, to take part. Mr Sussman dedicated to his cause, arms waving about in the air, dictating the pace, looking, searching for any hidden talent. I'm different now, narrowed down, focused, football my end game. Sussman the teacher, always rubbing his hands before instructing some boy towards improvement. Always one above the rest playing his instrument like a natural. Inspiration for Sussman the conductor, his baton striking the air with keen dedication as the stragglers follow a beat behind.

      My head turns without reason and I catch her face again, another side view, short hair, held. I'm caught by a moment of freeze, disheveled, her car accelerating away. I abandon my mates, scoop up my bag and scooter my bike into motion. Now firm on the saddle, I push harder, my bag not set in position bumps around behind. My friends left watching, deserted, not knowing the reason for my mute departure. There's a feeling of being taken over, something you must do, being out of control. My head down, my legs pumping as the pace picks up. I have a sighting but it's way ahead. I need some luck, my chances low, but she's held at the Red Lion crossing. I can feel my heart pumping, my body gaining heat, the sweat drop already forming on my brow. My left hand slips behind trying to set my troublesome load, my sack of books behaving like there's a monkey inside trying to escape. Excitement tingles my senses, my focus held by the car that carries her. She's away now heading along the river, up towards Mortlake, my home run. I make the Red Lion crossing and shoot across but I'm caught by a slowing bus, brakes needed cutting my speed. I pull around and need to gather speed, a slow gradient now zapping my progress as her car gains distance. The afternoon on the exercise course, football lunchtime, I feel the pinch of need but my tingle remains and drives me forward. She heads down Lower Mortlake a straight stretch of road, she pulls away. I feel loss but take a gamble, a short cut I know, a left passed the church, down the pathway, out near the level crossing at Sheen Lane, my last hope.

    I'm in luck, the gates are down as I approach Mortlake Station. The fast train throws a cooling breeze against my heated body as I halt in the side street. My mouth open, dry, sucking in the air, recovery time needed. I sit still, expectant, hopeful as the gates rise. My angled front wheel bumping against the curb, nervous perhaps as the cars start to cross. I take quick glances, like not wanting to be caught out in the open. What next anyway, no plan just spontaneous reaction, chasing a vision, my vision, legs in maroon boots. The cars thin out, she's not there, another route I suppose, a chance taken, not lucky this time. I need to gather myself, reluctant to vacate my mission. My front tyre still bumps the curb and I push harder now as anger rises, not like me at all. I swing my bag off my back and punch the troublesome books, just as well there's not a monkey inside. I'm lost somewhere, out of my usual zone, taken over by an invading force. I find my hand squeezing my nose as my front tyre continues showing its own frustration bumping away at the curb. I dismount and turn my bike, " sorry bike " I mumble as I try to gather myself. I wait still, half turned not wanting to admit defeat, collecting my thoughts, collecting myself. A cigarette butt flicks from the last car crossing, a signal perhaps a sign of defeat. It bounces then rolls towards me. I follow its slowing path as it judders to its end under my bike, a final hint of smoke to end its journey, to sign its end. I look down, butts everywhere, a dumping ground. The crossing forcing people to stop, five, ten minutes maybe. Must do something to fill the void. Tapping the fingers, fiddle with the radio, check the rear view mirror, still the addiction grips them. My father, a big man, solid, gripped by the drug. He rolls his own, methodical, the final lick to seal his need.

Sign of the times, Marlboro Man, Humphrey Bogart, advertising, planting the fast growing seeds of need in your brain. The addiction drawing the top off the weekly wage like their cold, wet, Friday night pint.

The gates closed again as the slow train pulls in. My head drops and I study the ground below, oil marks, fag ends, fag ends everywhere. I walk my bike, my companion, an unusual time for me I think but so is chasing after cars. I hear the train coming out of the station, gathering speed, heading I know for Clapham Junction. The route I use to Crystal Palace, Thursday nights, professional training for a chosen few. The train passes casting its usual breeze as it cuts through the air. I watch the windows, people looking out, talking perhaps, a newspaper up here and there, heads buried in the news of the day or perhaps just the page three photo. Off towards London the last carriage swaying side to side, the movement holds me, action, forces in motion. Like my running, I guess, able to move left or right up or down, the breeze passing over my face changing the tempo of my thoughts. Home I suppose, get the homework done first, routine, football at the back of the flats later with my mates. My focus not quite so solid something has moved, something not quite on the tracks.

I had been in my room since school, homework done, another two page story waiting for the red ink spider to do its corrections. It wasn't something I worried that much about, things I wasn't good at I looked upon as balanced out by the things you were good at. We can't all be writers or footballers, all tall or all small. Sometimes I think of things, an idea, a story line, I must write that down but it's gone before pen hits paper. My eyes glance over my work, good I think, the sensation of a hand again on my inner thigh.

A sweet sixteen birthday card greets me as I collect my homework books for school. No day off for birthday boy as I remove the folded one pound note from the happy card. There's not too much to a birthday anymore, the younger days, a parcel of surprise here, a parcel of surprise there. Now it's November, 1967, a cash donation in a card with spend it wisely written at the bottom. Spending it wisely could have multiple permutations for a sixteen year old adolescent boy.

Also a change in my routine tonight no football behind the flats killing the time before my parents get home. Tonight was different, Geoff Morris from school, a new teacher but also a football referee needing me to go with him to fix up a meeting. A neutral referee who I knew needed to cover our next school match against local rivals. Mum, yesterday already a bit anxious "But it's your birthday" she said as I tried to calm her with sixteen year old logic. Finally a head nod of agreement, nothing that special happening at home anyway. She returned to the kitchen, dinner to prepare, rituals of life, wake, work, eat, sleep. I mind Roger in the front room, my young brother only two years old, a late arrival to the family. A shock for my father she recalls, a smile always spreading across her face at the memory. We live on the top floor, four flights up. Rooftops spread away from our windows, in lines upwards towards the park. Houses, semi detached, detached, must be nice stepping into your front door without climbing four flights of steps first. Top of the Pops comes on, Roger's favourite half hour. He jigs and bends, mesmerised to the sounds, inherent I think from Mum. My food disappears too quickly from the plate, my hunger always present, growing too fast. Energy consumed at rapid rates, football, running, biking. I tidy my hair and look for smarter clothes. Not much choice in my wardrobe, basic things to get through the day. I settle as usual on my black polo neck, my for all occasions, can't say there was much of a choice. My hair looks good, fair, long as I study myself in the mirror. Long hair the sign of the times breaking away from the tidy short back and sides of the late fifties. The mirror holds my attention, I'm changing, radiant, a new young man, no longer the big boy. A smile crosses my face as I study my reflected image, features bigger, ears, nose, forehead. My eyes always blue but brighter, confident in my strength aware of my weaknesses. Good at some things, bad at others, acceptance, confidence in my life to live. Time to go now as I glance back and take one more look, a cocky kind of confident smile shines back at me.

    Morris's car, hot inside and there's a scent coming from some air freshener that dangles around gaining your attention as the bends appear. It tickles my nose, it's sharp scent adding to my discomfort, I'm not one who likes scented smells. The rain, steady and reliant as always beats its rhythm above. The wipers dragging my eyes from the scented freshener send out their own hypnotic drag on your senses. He makes small talk, asking too many questions, I don't know him well and return guarded answers. He's heavy set, carrying a stomach, not a helpful item when refereeing games, always wary of masters of the whistle. He wears a smile on his face, like the cat that got the cream. Not the open face of most of my teachers. I sense to be careful and change the talk to school items, much less personal. The journey's not long somewhere in Kingston, the skies are darkening as we pull into the rear car park. A small pub greets us as we manhandled the heavy sprung back door. Alcoves and corners to choose plus the highly magnetic pull of the open log fire that draws my immediate attention. A warmth springs forth adding to the room's comfort, shelter I think from the storm. Morris jabs my ribs, a pint of cold shandy placed in my hand, my attention still held by the flickering flames. Our contact is here, arrangements made as we sink further into our comfort chairs. More people filling the spaces, they occupy my attention, pubs still unfamiliar territory for me. I note their manner rhythms, arm and hand gestures to emphasise their points to hold their audience in wait for the punch line. A little over play as the alcohol begins to play its part, adding extra relief I guess from a tough day at the office. A smoke haze builds, many sucking in the witches brew of addiction. Black smoke, their cigarette ends flare, a second or two wait before exhaling, adding their share to the haze above. My chair has absorbed me, I was comfortable, relaxed, resting, the shandy beer perhaps a little help. Morris was occupied with his new friend, tales of a referee's life, their bond, uniting them in immediate friendship, I was

sitting next to two whistle blowers. My neck began to warm as my polo neck tightened, my eyes closed, the fire light attraction tiring them a little, I rested. Perhaps I slept for a moment but I'm not sure but I felt the mood change, hellos and welcomes as my eyes opened. There before me, the maroon boots blocking out the fire. A burning heat swept through me setting my fingers and toes on fire. My gaze was held, an arms distance away she stood, her arms reaching out, hands held backwards soaking up the fire heat. I straightened held by her presence. A rear view, tight top again enhancing slim limbs. A short tasseled leather skirt holding shapely legs. A presence surrounded her, an air of confidence, purpose, pose, a little aware perhaps of her effect. She turned rubbing her toasted hands together, her fingers enhanced by long slender nails looking white and delicate under a shiny coat of nail polish. Her face round, red cheeks, brown eyes smiling down at me. I felt I was moving, gathering speed, propelled along by an invisible force. Wind blowing, my clothes, my hair, my nerve endings tingling my body.
"I'm Eve," she said, " pleased to meet you." Her hand reached down, a coldness still held her fingers. My mind trying to locate with my tongue. Her touch absorbing all my senses, the depth in

her eyes filling my mind with unanswered questions.
" Ross" I managed to squeeze out as her fingers left my hand. She held my eyes like she could read them, somewhere lost in space. A bill board on Time Square, I Love You, I Love You, going round and around in my head.

I should have stood, I thought, a chance lost as she moved off to join the clan. Other chairs were poached as Tom Madison approached with loaded glasses. I straightened from my slumber, attention required now, my vision seated close. The earlier attractions just a backstage to the woman I now gazed upon. Talking immediately she gained centre ground only pausing as her drink was handed down. I remained held in my chair a little out of the circle totally absorbed by her movements, her hands so delicate wavering in the air to emphasise her statements . It was not my scene, out of my comfort zone. I felt like an interloper someone peeping through the crack of the door. Her confidence radiated out and infected the others into serious debate. Like bees around a honey pot eager to participate, a new injection of debate. Discussion, different views all added up to make the whole. New to me, no discussion of events in our house. Meals taken off to sit in front of the TV. Not even a " How was your day "

Topics, news, school, all got placed under the hammer, the hum of input, worked on, dissected, agreement, disagreement, a truce to defer. I watched her transfixed, forcing myself to look away only so I could glance back again. She held me captured, rolling about in her web, everything else way down the importance ladder. I caught her eye as she looked up, she rubbed her arm and looked down at her watch adjusting the face a little between her delicate fingers and then a deeper gaze returned. My hand reached to remove a lock of hair fallen over my face, my eyes held by hers. The loose hair twisted in my fingers a nervous response to cover my beating heart. Our eyes locked, a moment in time, a new experience, a demanding force. What could I read in those sparking brown eyes holding my focus. It was only a moment but its effect had traveled deep inside me. Something strong and demanding, a message, searching for a rock. Her story not all light and well being, a need for truth and honesty. A heat shot through me and turned my neck into fire coals. The polo neck gripping me increasing the heat, itching against my neck. I swing up, veering away towards the gents, escape, escape, regroup.

My top lay bundled to the side, my body bare as I splashed my face with water. My cheeks red with the excitement that gripped my mind. Nothing else mattered she had me hook line and sinker. I'd known girlfriends before , kiss and cuddle, mess around a bit, nothing serious. No more polo necks in pubs I thought as I prepared for a better round two. Morris was standing, "OH, there you are, time to take you back."

" I'm OK, not yet," a pleading I could hear in my voice.

" No, " he said giving Eve the eye," Time to go,"
I looked into her eyes as they strayed towards me.

" See you again," I said with more courage than I felt.

"Yes, yes," she said looking away a little too quickly, an extra blush I thought covering her cheeks. I made the heavy set back door and gave it an extra kick as it flew open, the car park looking dark and uninviting. The cold blustering wind hit me sending a shudder through my rampant senses. A storm around my body indeed to match the storm in my mind.

" Eve insisted I take you home," said Morris as our car doors shut in unison.

" Your parents, she thought would be concerned,"

The time, fiddling with her watch, I thought. She was aware, protecting me, fidgeting a bit with worry, that's what it was.

I lay flat in bed, my eyes closed, the evenings events played, rewind, played again. An ear bashing from my parents for being late but they soon settled on seeing birthday boy's safe return. Any later and they would have been up the school in the morning, perhaps it being my sixteenth birthday had weakened their case. Saved by the bell or something else, perhaps an angel, a time for this a time for that. I lay still, the shape I dissected, slowly up, slowly down. The maroon boots a little worn, zips up the inside just short of the knee. Their worn crease lines adding character, style, setting a new trend, fashion, sexuality. Black fish net tights doing their job to perfection, tight around her slender knees and disappearing under the leather tassels hanging from her skirt. A sexual allure from her neat muscled thigh, the lines of her body clear defined by her style, new, absorbing, challenging. Her short cut hair, a challenge to the times, allowing the features of her face to radiate out. Dark eyebrows, high set, eyes shining with knowledge, confidence and a message. My own body energised like a new being occupied it's core. Delicate, sensitive nerve endings tingling all over, a longing to process even capture the object of my desire. Was it there or was it only my longing, my need that summoned up the challenge. This is me, Eve, if you want me come and get me.

Did I miss anything? All recorded for replay like my new Beatles record. I know all the words, I think I did not miss anything. " She loves you and you know that can't be bad." I'm going to try' try' try. It was late, somewhere there I fell asleep, on the up or on the down, I fell!

I was somewhere along Thornton Heath High Street my kit bag slung over my shoulder playing its usual tricks of constant annoyance. I knew it was me not the bag, it didn't weigh much but instead of being a silent problem it was like a disgruntled child pulling at your hand. The day had been long at school and I think I spent most of the time studying the many small, square glass windows that allowed the sunlight to enter the classrooms. My thoughts were varied and strange jumping about from kicking a ball around to looking for the possible hidden detail of something I had missed from the night before. Eyes so clear, the colour brown hinting at mischief and adventure. Living at a different level, talking, debate, finding agreement to a new road forward, why this and why that, so different and intriguing. Different by far from the track I had been on, tucked away on the top floor of Montgomery House.

A fresh gust of wind carrying an added chill returned my focus to the evening ahead. I had set off soon after school, of course there had been the looking around, searching for my vision but Thursday night was training night with little time to spare. A good ride home to pickup my kit and devour any food that was available and head for Mortlake Station. I was soon en route for Chatham Junction the train pulling away over the crossing where I had waited with such disturbed impatience just a few days back. The usual stumped faces stared back from the waiting cars, with tapping fingers and flaring fag ends. I knew that it was match night, practice match, show us what you're got night. Getting near the end of the season, new boys needed to fill the apprenticeship quota for Crystal Palace football club. I had been at Brentford FC for a little while which was our local club and one my father supported but they had terminated their youth policy for lack of funds. Arthur Row had spotted me playing at a district match and invited me to train at the Palace. I had been going there for a while and the journey was now imprinted on the back of my hand. The last section was a stiff walk up Whitehorse Lane where the wind blew even more and the main stand grew bigger, more impressive with every step. The nerves kicked in a bit now as the challenge draws nearer, tested, tested and tested again. I have a confidence that holds me firm, I know the game, the moves, the rules. My body could use extra weight but I'm growing too fast, a hunger that's always there. The need for energy, those chocolate bars that taste so good, always trying to make them last, slowly sucking on the rich chocolate. Mars Bars, Picnic's and the new Topic with those tasty hazel nuts inside. I'll buy one after, definitely, just enough money in my pocket after I get my travelling expenses. There's a coldness to the next gust of wind as my eyes set on the looming stadium. Another test for the spring chicken, the one who wants to be a footballer, the one who will be a footballer. Just get out there and show then what you've got "Boyo". It's hard to find a spare hook in the changing room so I settle in a corner with my clothes in a disordered pile. The air buzzes as multiple shapes and sizes of youth in the making shed their clothes. The team sheets hang on the wall causing a gathering of eager attention. I remain seated, set in my ways, time needed to get focused, under the microscope again tonight. I watch as the white shirts, the red shirts start to cover the jiggling bodies, plenty of subs tonight. Jenkins is there, white, the number 9 front runner for the team. There's been a change lately, a movement from the lone centre forward to twin strikers. Winning the World Cup has changed the tactics, team co-ordination and balance over individual efforts. I don't talk, there's enough of that already, breathe deep and prepare. Most kids like to jump around like they have ants in their pants talking ten to the dozen. Not my way at all, I enter my space were it's quiet as the white cardboard shirt works its stubborn way over my head. There is a shake in my knees as a slight shiver runs through my body. Small goose bumps cover my arms and legs as my studs start tapping on the polished floor. It's time for me to move, get out of this honey pot. I stand stretching as a sea of heads cover my eye line. It's not far to the door but it's a zigzag route tonight. I pass Erne Wally our trainer, Welsh to the core, a hard man but fair. You do what I tell you man or you get a good smack. Our eyes meet, an understanding there in the moment, it translates as it's time to show us what you've got. A whispered "do your stuff tonight boyo," slips from his lips. His muscular body a credit to hard work and dedication to the game, do the best you can with what you've got written all over his face, his motto. I give back a nod, an understanding there, a lot unsaid just known in the circles of physical effort, eye contact and comradeship, a true team player. I take a big breath as I hit the corridor, the air sharper filling my body, setting my mind as my eyes focus on the end of the tunnel. Challenges set, things to overcome, to get done, life's road, your life's journey. I see her again, the walk across the playground, the purpose, body set to sort a problem, the head high, mind clear, do a good job tonight it's time to perform. It sets my mind, I straighten my back, breathe deep, a smaller shiver now as the cold outside air works its own sneaking passage through the tunnel. Many heads now bobbing about, the wait always a problem, time to fill, scratch your itch, pull up your socks, re-tuck your shirt, the test awaits. I pull on my sleeves but there's no warmth there just a white cardboard cover with a 9 on the back, but it's my 9, the number I want. Some lights now show a fine drizzle which accompanies the gusts of circling wind. A few more seconds pass before the OK is given to the assortment of bouncing heads. We enter the pitch. The empty stands loom up both sides hanging over us like giant voids, each end the terracing reaching up into the sky. A cold darkness surrounding the glowing pitch as the rain fades, the stage is set, the whistle soon to blow, the whistle. It's different all the training, the running, the practice needed to achieve the required end product. It comes down to the whistle that cuts the air and sets the game in motion. To be able to perform, to hold it together, to make the pass that counts, to see the pass that counts. My body responds to the surge within. I eat up the ground as my legs open up. There's a new spring there, my studs secure in the moist ground as I make the runs that count. A give and go which opens up a clear effort on goal which requires an athletic save from the goalkeeper. I give instructions to my other players organising a more constructed attack. The time is fleeting as the half time whistle blows causing me to wonder where the 45 minutes went. Time that flies when all that matters is the moment twenty two players are totally consumed, real life to be resumed. I stroll off the pitch my body fit, stronger I sense, more in the bank for the second half. My warm breath cuts the air then turns into a haze I walk through heading for the tunnel. I notice a group of bobbing heads way up in the stand, Bert Head, the manager and all casting their eye over the potential talent. There's a buzz as the teams are rearranged, I sit enjoying the sensation that runs through me. My body strong, fit, mind over matter ready to go again. Erni Walley drifts pass, "Take a shower and rest up, boyo," he says "see you next week." I lean back and close my eyes, my confidence confirmed, a good job done tonight.

A week had passed in a haze of unrest, school routine continued its journey to occupy the young minds but somehow I had moved outside the hub. My mind was alive buzzing with a growing confused need. Knowing all the short cuts and back alleys had helped. I had made progress, hit a goal, my speedy bike had found the house of my vision, it was close. I had found where she lived and waited hidden. A terrace house over the railway line only two roads along from my nan's house, familiar territory for me. I stood at a distance, hidden, nervous in my stance as my head lent forward to see her arrive and park the car in one swift reverse. She was out, a basket bag swinging at her side as her assorted keys opened number 10. A young boy as well juggling his small school bag followed. My eyes flitting about, had I been seen how does one act normal when all your senses crash into each other. The discomfort grew, a rising stack of agitation, had I been seen?
Is a neighbour eyeing me now, spying from his window, noticing my discomfort, witnessing strange behaviour? Time to go, I made a quick left heading back to the railway line. My head wanting to turn, look again, in need of a connection, eye contact, a gesture, recognition

of something different. I skipped up the steps to cross over the railway line. The fast train hit me with its usual expected gust of heated air splattering my long hair across my eyes. Movement, train, wheels, wind, a butterfly here a bird there. There's something about it, the co-ordination that attracts me, always has, many moments just standing on the bridge waiting for the next train to make its swaying journey under my feet and send up its greeting gust of wind. The sheer energy, power of movement envelops me, the warm gust soon replaced by the cold evening air as another winter's night hangs ready to creep into your bones. I follow the wind circles as they pick up fallen leaves along South Worple Way heading towards me. The movement I watch with fascination like the clouds always coming from the west. The circles of wind with their assortment of flying leaves wrap themselves around me searching for openings to feed off my body heat. My coat is prepared no gaps are found, and the twirling air moves on in search of more unprepared victims. The train has passed but its journeys never ending, ten minutes, twenty minutes how far away will it be then working hard delivering the relentless demands of the workforce. I stand there now my hands firm on the handrail. I pull it and push it flexing my muscles but it remains solid, unperturbed, undisturbed by my mounting frustration. Please bring another train I want another train to occupy my thoughts. The usual passers, mostly mothers that work their prams efficiently up the stairs and down the stairs. Their daily routine over the railway bridge, kids to school, kids to Richmond park, kids to shops, kids back home. They don't linger like me. No time to spare on the family ladder, homes to reach, time always at a premium. I look down the stairs as a cautious mother takes hold of her child's hand, guidance needed, time to cross the road. Bob's Store still there planted on the corner, ideally located, sweets and ice cream posters on the door window waiting for the next victim of need, the advertising guarantees a sure way to boost profits. I recall many trips there trading the extra vegetables from my father's allotment for other much needed goods and of course that chocolate bar that must be eaten. My younger days come to mind in Bob's corner shop, delivering newspapers over the bridge and back again to get a few coins in the pocket for weekend treats. Knowing every route, every back alley, every bump of a young man's journey. Even though I remain here a while there's no feeling of doing something suspicious it's familiar ground just taking my time watching trains, shooting the breeze. An eye may be on me now from a passerby, no problem, I'm not spying on my desire, no twitching of nerve endings now. The longing remains a growing pursuit, a drive that takes command, swamps your body leaves reason way behind. My hands gripping harder now the last bit of to-ing and fro-ing on the cold, solid, rock steady hand rail.

The big match tomorrow sneaks it way into my crowded mind, a win tomorrow puts us in number one spot to win the league. No doubt we are upsetting the establishment, the bigger schools usually share the prize. Us, the underdogs challenging the status quo. That's why you have competition, all sports, all games, a deep need to motivate, driven, to be challenged to be a winner, the underdog must have his day. I love the game, mental control needed, to kick a ball, to score a goal, the movement, foresight, the body, mind, totally absorbed in the challenge. All efforts focused on one aim, the ball that hits the back of the net. My head leans forward to stretch my neck, a chill has entered, my lingering too long, it's time to retreat, regroup, time to go home.

The next morning I pedal hard to school, I'm running late. I like a comfort zone time to look, time to watch, time to access. It's a grim shadowy morning, the river flow so high, its rising water looking mysterious and daunting.

The River Thames testing its banks, the tides immense power rolling in, rolling out. You feel it must overflow, a monster not easily contained its daily high tide line not quite enough to burst its banks. The long brick wall on Lonsdale Road holding back the creeping monster. The wall solid its strength tested daily by the silent moving force. It holds my attention as I traverse the last stretch to school. My rhythm good, legs working but holding cruise control, always a bit in the bank for later. The usual head up searching as I stash my bike, the walk slow, looking, observing as I finally enter the bruised wooden doors into school. A morning to pass before the challenge of the afternoon football match.

I'm not quite sure where the morning went, I had notes in my bag and homework to do but recalling the time line left me stumped. I knew my body was preparing itself for the afternoon game, focus and concentration needed in heavy supplies for the challenge had arrived yet again. My team mates gathered around our usual pre-match corner of the play ground. A quiet place that had become our bonding corner. Habits that present themselves, the wire netting to pull, a post or two to tap or kick as we stand expressing our nervous preparation habits. Various bags holding our kit, our school colours to cover our backs yet again. Team members, brothers in arms as we wait fiddling to control the growing challenge once again. To win, rise to the top, be important, be somebody. Our place to gather, to be one, united in our task. Could we actually win the league? Challenges are always there, can you blow out in one breath the growing number of candles on your birthday cake? Can you write a story without a spelling mistake? We stood bonded, waiting for our assortment of teachers with cars to ferry us along to the Black Horse. No school bus for us, expenses kept to a minimum, a school on its last legs one could say.

        The greyness of the early morning had led to a good downpour of rain before the reliable westerly winds had started to move on the low hanging grey clouds. I stood now on the soft ground, boots in hand checking conditions, a good stud required to give a secure footing for the contest ahead. The dressing room was cramped, always a vast amount of space outside but no room to spare inside? We jiggled and wriggled about till our school colours hung from our assorted bodies. A build up of spent energy had taken the chilly edge off the room temperature, our young bodies, hearts pounding were adjusting to the unsaid, unquestioned demand yet again. It was time to play, to perform again as we trailed out to the challenge of the whistle blower. The tops of buses caught my eye moving along the high boundary wall heading into Richmond, the upstairs passengers eyeing us as we lined up for kick off. The game was governed by the sticky conditions kick it long and close down the gaps. We just made halftime holding our opponents at one one. They had shaped up well giving Sooty and Sweep a tough time at the back. Failure to get good crosses into the box had reduced our effectiveness. My game had been disturbed some tough sliding tackles had kept me quiet. Perhaps my mind was not fully focused, full concentration had gone for a walk. The half time sliced oranges rapidly disappeared as Robby waved his arms about trying to stimulate his rugged , shivering clan into more positive territory. Exposed arms and legs gathering more goose bumps as Robby's rallying demands struggled to do their job. The cloudy sky lost its hold as rays of low sunlight shone across our assorted group of adolescence. A sudden change of mode, time to go to work, time to make it happen. The second half started fast with many changes of procession, we were doing the work, not the ball. Things settled as I caught the ball just right and its circling momentum found the top corner of the goal. It was a signal for me, a sign that cleared the mind, get focused take control now! The goal we all want to score had taken the wind out of our opponents, their passing going astray, tired limbs making tired minds, their team set up began to fall short. A late goal secured a good win for us, we had maintained our momentum, the end game, upsetting the hierarchy was still in our grasp.

As usual the dressing room was given scant attention many clothes bundled into bags, our school colours still covering our backs looking to be washed at home. Perhaps a jumper or light coat to keep out the chill as the sun lost its power as the last rays of light sent stretching shadows over the ground. We hovered like lost children around the entrance gates waiting for our teacher taxi's to ferry us home. A couple of lads were sucking on their Mars Bars getting envious glances from the rest of their team mates. A telling reminder to bring Mars Bars for the next match. Morris pulled in first, his cat that gets the cream smile slowly covering his reddening face as his eyes glanced over the waiting clan. I held back as his swinging scent package attracted my eye. My teammates bumbled in his car without hesitation, his tyres sitting lower as the last door slammed shut. He pulled away with a jolt from the gear box, more rev's needed and perhaps a little more concentration as well to carry his extra load.

    Four of us were left shuffling about from one foot to the other, team tactics became the conversation topic, how to win, how we just won, adjust the tactics to suit the player's abilities. I got well involved in this debate and did not notice as the Morris Minor pulled to a halt behind me. "Get in quick lads I don't have much time." I turned to see the face of my desire. I stood stumped as my team mates piled in the back seat causing the car to rock from side to side. A soft scent hit my nose as I sat heavy on the front seat causing a sharp cramp to seize my hamstring muscle. I rubbed hard on the stricken area this only adding more to my total unease. My knees seemed to occupy any available space sticking up prominently it seemed adding a shake of their own to my troubled mind. My hands rested on them trying to defuse their nervous discontent. Her hand moved up towards me shaving my arm, " Are you alright, Ross" she asked. My name remembered on her lips left me stunned and stumped, what to say "Yes miss, Yes Eve ." " I'm OK " finally snaked its way out.

Her touch on my arm had left its presence like a warm spot on a cold night. My left hand moved up to cover the touch, searching I think but definitely too late to find its goal. The tingle from her fingers remains like the itch you cannot see. I wished her hand was still there touching me ever so lightly. I found myself looking at her fully absorbing the creature that had captured my heart. The soft scent I had noticed before had gathered strength, its unseen agreeable presence tickled my nostrils. Her eyes, brown, shining, were back on the road, concentration needed to get her assorted clan of adolescent boys back to camp.

"Thanks for picking us up, miss" finally passed my lips as I gathered myself to take advantage. The time getting shorter with every passing traffic light. I talked about my wish to be a footballer and training at Crystal Palace. The words seemed to roll out, still nervous definitely but occupying the silent, unwanted void that had existed before. She showed interest, a smile crossed her face and a welcome light in her eye that encouraged my ramblings. We had arrived back at school in record time it seemed, a deserted playground greeted us, its size impressive without the scattering of adolescent kids to fill its fenced boundaries. The back seaters had already jumped out heading over to the bike shed. They were free of the obsession that gripped me. Had I spoken too much, rattled on a bit I suppose, my nerves winning the day. I climbed out my long legs stretching, enjoying again the freedom of space. My kit bag caught on something under my seat. I had to lean down to unfasten the snag. I felt my face reddening to the challenge, the closeness of her body my eye line low a different viewpoint, again ruling mind into disorder. Looking up I felt a change, a moment there when I looked up into her face. Was I reading it right? Neither of us moved as our eyes locked. I was low looking up, she was still, quiet, no words spoken, two people held by the moment lost I hoped in each other's eyes. My hand below still moving around but its purpose lost, the snag still there but doing its job perfectly joining us together as one. "I need to go," she said "I have to collect my son." her voice sounded nervy like she was troubled. Our eyes slowly, unwillingly certainly on my part withdrew, "Thanks Eve" left my lips as my eyes left hers. I stood motionless watching as her car drifted away. I wanted it again that feeling her car to come back, to look into her eyes again, strange, disorientation, her mind perhaps in turmoil like mine. I tried to find her car again, looking searching but it had been absorbed into the hub of the early rush hour. Somehow I was holding my bike how it had got from the bike shed to me remains a mystery to this day of putting pen to paper. The school caretaker stood waiting, waving his impressive band of keys in the air. It took me a moment to realise he wanted me outside the gate so he could lock up. "Good result again today" passed his lips as the lock clicked efficiently into place. It shook me back from my fantasy world, the school caretaker was also aware we were making waves.

    A heavy gust of early evening wind caught me by surprise as I stood trying to be back in the present. It carried a nasty chill, its journey along the river probably adding the extra bite to its tail. I rummaged in my bag for warmer covers, exposed legs even for the young certainly not a good idea. It was December, the sinking sun already hidden by thickening clouds. Christmas around the corner, another week to master modern maths, XY and Z, not possible sprung to mind as I felt the cheeky smile return across my face. The thought brought me back to reality, time to get home back into some kind of groove. There was hope there, the way her eyes shone, my desire responding, warm and welcoming, I felt sure, confident or was that just wishful thinking of a young man's heart. I need to step up to the challenge, there was no way out for me, I want her badly. The stirring thoughts of holding her close, my arms around her, the driving need to kiss those soft inviting lips, could it happen, could it?

With bike in hand I walked for a while, chain clicking, wheels spinning accompanying my settling mind. The old reservoirs over to my right, fishing after school comes to mind knowing where the removable iron rail is that allows easy access. Many hours after school spent there a few years back chasing the elusive prized carp that hides itself so well. Often having to be satisfied with perch that always seemed easily tempted by a wiggling worm or maggot. My mind was roaming, the last few years moving like a whirlwind, things I used to do, caught up in adolescence but always that football to be kicked. The challenge to hit the spot, the target on the wall, practice to make perfect, the sweet feel of the ball as it leaves your foot. The position of movement that's so important, to make the space, timing, to know when to fill it to your advantage. Taken up by a changing music world, the Stones, the Beatles leading the followers as they stride out yet again for the number one position. I play their songs all the time filling in the gaps when school and football have run their course for the day. Always something new on the music scene challenging the status quo. The changing, suggestive lyrics expressing the sexual freedom of the times. Mini skirts with tight braless tops outlining the female shape as they jiggle around on Top of the Pops. My record player always on the go, its volume turned up to stifle out my own out of tune words as I sing along to my latest purchase, " I want to hold your hand, I want to hold your hand." The wish to be able to sing in tune and hope you will enjoy the show but again for me it comes down to XY and Z.

My extra clothes had stopped the bite of the evening air but the light was going as I passed under the train bridge. The thickening waters of the Thames added to the feeling that winter had returned its firm hold again. The people passing their heads low, covered in layers of winter clothes blown about by the passing lorries and buses that barely have room to pass through the old style opening. Clear evidence showing high up in the deep scratch marks that many didn't judge it well. It was time to ride my trusted bike not push it anymore. The walk had worked giving me time to return to earth. My mind was set, I had no choice, something had been planted inside me, a new goal definitely awaited me, and it had a name, its name was Eve.

The last week at school drifted by, the lessons mostly revisiting territory covered before. The brains of the young waiting to escape the confines of the school fence, a three week break from Robby's whistle of command and the squeaky chalk marks upon the blackboard. To return refreshed with studious homework that reflected a dedicated attempt to impress. To show willingness for the final run up to exams, to be graded, O level for me A level for the so called sharper minded. Training at Crystal Palace also had its Christmas break so the back of the flats was revisited often to pass the many hours that school and training normally absorbs. My mates gathering often, the chat lines, whose with who, the local girls always fidgeting about, giggling amongst themselves, waiting for any new kid to appear on the block. Frequent trips to the local dump along the river, always looking for bike bits to improve or smarten up your ride. The workers helpful and considerate down there, they put all the bike bits to one side for the local kids to hunt out any usable bits. The path along the river getting to the dump always an adventure, a tree to climb, a hideaway camp to build from the many bits of debris left stranded at low tide. It was familiar ground that route along the Thames. You knew the bumps, the up and downs and especially those muddy puddles that presented the challenge. Could you get through the mud hole without getting stuck. Your life on the bike always a challenge, to take the back routes, to disappear up the park, to ride those sticky, tricky mud holes. A lot of time was spent like that doing the usual challenges of being young but I was a little out of sink. I had tried my best, my casual attempts to pass her house, to linger at the kerb for extra seconds pretending that something was amiss with my bike chain. The car not parked neatly against the kerb, the house lights not shining at night. Failing attempts to spot my desire. It was holiday time, Christmas, another place must be hiding her away. Many thoughts crowded my mind, I examined myself, some moments I lay still on my bed gazing at the ceiling. I was used to action, busy, moving to the next challenge, the itch that wouldn't go, laying still an unusual occurrence for me. Ideas entered for examination, was it possible, the need to be with her, was I fooling myself into a fantasy world. My world of football, music, biking and mates taken over by a repeating vision. My body restless upon the bed, legs bent, legs straight, hands active searching for the unseen itch. Following the new crack in the ceiling that I hadn't noticed before. Its zig zag journey holding your gaze, mapping its route from one wall to another as you again brush the fallen hairs from your face. Your hand stays on your head your hair held tight by the closing fingers. You pull a bit, to create feeling, to get a response, your nerves, senses moving you on to firmer ground. You know you have to try again there's no way out of the tangled web that's captured your mind and body. She is my desire, Eve will be my desire.

I had made a move, selected a Christmas card from the assortments of sizes and words of good will to all at this very special time of year. A small thing perhaps but it was all I could think of to fill the " Nobody Here " message of the closed curtains. You would think it a straight forward easy challenge but my mind was not decisive. It pondered over the many phrases that laid prominent upon the white shiny cards. What words would suit? did they offer the pretence of hidden meanings? It was after a tangled moment of indecision that the simple card won the day, "Merry Christmas". I needed to add something, definitely, a suggestion perhaps, could we meet, have a chat, perhaps even a coffee at the corner shop? My confidence was having trouble as I stared down upon my pen hovering just above "Merry Christmas". Thoughts of the red ink spider played their hand as I looked around for practice paper. Laying out a few words helped but that elusive hidden meaning would not surface. I kept it simple "Wishing you and your son a very special Christmas, Ross, PS thanks again for the lift." Of course the next part was to post it, I know no one was living in the house lately, its curtains closed to the many passing strangers heading to the shops along the Upper Richmond Road. I rode my bike, passing a couple of times those light blue doors, the number ten burning its memory forever into my brain. It was time to act I stowed by bike against the kerb, pushed open the iron gate that had seemed such a barrier before and the card in my hand disappeared without question or hesitation through the slot. I stood hovering a moment my nerves tingling, I felt close to her, I was on her property my card delivered lying in wait inside for her return. She would see it, pick it up, look at my words. What would go through her mind, would she recall me hunting for the snag that held my bag, our eyes meeting, could she read what was written there. Did she also feel something that overrules the brain, was she taken by surprise? Where to go now back over the railway bridge, linger a bit, pull on the rails as the fast train to Waterloo sends up its blast of wintery air. It brings you back to the present, settles you a bit, to think your message lies inside her house. It is a message more than just a contact isn't it? Will she see it that way, look over the words a few times instead of just planting it on the shelf with all the others? To get collected up in a week or two, its life span short, soon time to hit the rubbish bin as another Xmas passes you along life's journey. Will she see the hidden words that reflect my aching heart, to take that extra moment to examine my few shaky written words. Will the card plant a seed, to recall that look of longing, to note the desperation of a young man's heart. Did she see it, register that moment of something special as I looked up the other day to be lost in those sparkling brown eyes. The wisdom, knowledge there, clever, intelligent, definitely a handful for the other teachers to bounce their ideas off. I recall the pub in Kingston where she held court, the centre of the hub. Where the others gathered around, drawn to debate their topics, all eager to have their say. Like bees to a honey pot an attraction that floats its magic upon the air. The radiance of her sexuality attracting glances from outside her own clan of activity. The sideways glances from the standing men as their pints rise higher to hide their sneaking glances at the sitting attraction. My own loss of control sending me to boiling point a memory that will live with me forever.

    I was in the back seat of my Dad's car with my two brothers, Steven the first son in centre position with Roger in his Sunday best on the other side. It was Boxing Day, the extended family get together day. We were off to Feltham to my Dad's mums house, Nanny Feltham we called her. Boxing Day was the aunts and uncles unite day of the year. There were eight of them in total so many siblings like us were the result of their various partnerships. Not much talking went on in our car as our gazes were set to view the passing activities from our cramped back seat. Yesterday had been a wet Christmassy day so our family time had been spent viewing the TV specials that had been advertised weeks before as must see programmes over the holiday period. Various wrappings and gift boxes took up any available space on our limited shelves. Dad always seemed to get toiletries or socks, limited money made for limited presents. He had done his extra butchery work down Sheen Lane, skills he had learnt in his army days. He got the pick of the turkeys and a bit extra of this and that, mum was skilled at making available food last a few more days. I had slipped out around mid day when a slight brightening of the sky encouraged my desperation to pass her house again. It had been fruitless, no change in those curtains, their exact positioning imprinted on my brain like my face on a favourite photo. I had lingered, not wanting to leave, even sat on her wall a while pretending to fidget with a problem on my bike cable. Somehow entering her gate and posting the Xmas card had broken an invisible barrier. My confidence was running on high as I imagined it still lying in wait upon her passage floor. Was she also thinking about me, had I infected her the same way, was she troubled with a mind in disarray. Did she want to see me as well, was the longing inside her as desperate as mine. Had she also been taken over, possessed even like me by a driving need. The questions kept on coming adding to a confusion building in my brain. Her brick wall seat had become uncomfortable as my fidgeting increased, it was definitely time to move on. I was met by highs and lows all the way home. Was I fooling myself to think that I could have infected her in the same way? She was alone I felt sure her previous partnership gone off the tracks. A young child to take care of trying to find a firm footing to move forward. Finding herself parked up at Barnes Boys School a little away from the social, educational, climbing ladder. Obviously a mature educated woman with a young child, much more in tune with the ways of the world than me for sure. I lingered on my railway bridge, its calming presence helping to regroup my senses. I felt strong, there was something inside me different from before. I had moved on, a feeling like football behind the flats had ran its course. I was looking elsewhere now, my destiny had laid a path for me to walk, it was up to me to follow the signs to reach its end. In such a short period of time my viewpoint was clearer, more positive, the feeling I had left a certain stage of my youth behind. The sudden gust from the thickening clouds sent a clear signal that the rains were about to return. The stinging edge of winter's chill always a reminder to take shelter from the storm. It was time to return home, the Christmas specials would be starting soon. My exit was swift, the slippery down steps of the bridge no problem for a sixteen year old boy. His loyal bike bouncing by his side, who was totally sweated away by an unseen, unstoppable force. I had moved on my life now at a turning point. My focus was set, a different goal to seek had entered my life and laid down its challenge.

      We were well passed Richmond as I returned mentally to the present. There was a brightening to the sky which added promise to the thought of escaping my Nan's house with all my cousins. They had their own kick about area where the Boxing Day annual football match carried a lot of kudos around the neighbourhood. Any disputes were quickly settled in the old fashion way leaving everyone to be careful with their tackles or verbal comments. A couple of my cousins were well known and respected in this area so normally a good game was had by all. This time out burning up our youthful reserves left the grown ups to catch up on all the news and of course a hefty amount of drink was consumed by the time we returned. The increase in volume on the music box soon had them waltzing around the floor. I observed my mother, she was slim, her long brown hair dangling down but held firm at the back by a shining clasp. Her loose hanging dress emphasising her flowing movement as she twisted and turned. My father solid by her side, the male, the female, a partnership made official they say by a walk up the aisle, a ring on the finger, a photo to remember followed by the signed wedding certificate. They had met on Richmond Bridge one sunny day in springtime. My mother and her friend were licking on the must have ice cream of the day, the cone firmly held to avoid losing any of the valuable vanilla ice cream. My dad and his mate just back from Burma on leave were passing and said " Give us a lick then girls" and that you could say was that. So now I'm here with my two brothers watching them taking centre ground on the dance floor. My parents held your attention, the way their eyes met and then swivelled away. Their bodies in sequence, a chemistry of mixed ingredients that had gelled them together in thought and movement. I was caught by this idea, many here were on their second or even third marriage which had added a mixed assortment of cousins. Did they experience the driving need to connect that gripped me now, was their need the same, where they taken over, out of control? If so why did it end? What happened to that driving force that rules body over mind. Did love buy a ticket and leave the station? Does love leave town as suddenly as it arrived? How could it end, it couldn't end, I was sure mine couldn't end. I had been totally overrun by these thoughts for a while even the ice in my drinking water had melted. The temperature was mounting as I finally returned my thoughts to observe the growing family unity, another Christmas and good will to all. Other slow starters were now vying for any available space as the waltzing music started to lose ground under the challenge of rock and roll with of course that injection of Elvis the pelvis. I found myself swaying on the spot as the hum of family unity gathered. "Well, bless my soul what's wrong with me, I'm shaking like a leaf on an old oak tree" My grandmother held centre ground she had been half pulled and half pushed into the centre of the dance floor. She was jigging about her movements not so refined as she caught the happy encouraging looks on the faces of her grown children. Her clan of eight had surrounded her, their arms and legs moving to their own individual rhythm of the music. Their strong bond of unity renewed, a testament to family values as the rest of us siblings were absorbed by the atmosphere, Boxing Day 1967 was definitely one of the best.

I had taken to my bike to challenge the many hours of waiting that existed before school started again. It was a strange contrast normally you didn't want school to start but it had always raced towards you with increasing downhill speed. Now for me the wait seemed endless like time was on a severe uphill climb. How many times could you pass her door without suspicion mounting in any observant neighbour peering from his window as that young man on his bike just went passed again. Had I lingered there again perhaps a little too long, how many times could a bike chain need adjusting. That sitting on the wall shooting the breeze look on my face, perhaps I was a little more confident as I pictured my card face up with "For Eve" prominently written. The rest from continual football and training had refreshed my reserves of energy. My bike travelled better over the many bumpy tracks that attracted and dictated my routes. Palewell Park, Sheen Common and Richmond Park all absorbed those long hours of waiting. I took more time to observe my surroundings the trees with their bare branches reaching to the sky. Another spring around the corner to cover them once again in a sea of green leaves. A few rabbits perched on their back legs nibbling away at spartan food. Their watchful eyes scanning for that sneaky fox that knows its territory so well. The air fresh sucked into my lungs, my breathing controlled, my heart sound as it pumped the oxygen to feed my working body. I felt strong, my cruise speed maintaining momentum even up the stiffest of climbs. I wondered if my mates were missing me, I had not visited the back of the flats or even passed that way on my biking routes. Heavy rains had halted my travels nearing the return to school slowing the ticking clock even more. You spent time with your nose pressed against the cold window pane as your heated breath smeared out a growing circle. The circular heart shape drawn out with 'EVE' clearly written in the middle with two watery kiss signs underneath. Its visual presence occupying your thoughts " Oh to kiss those lips?" Would you float away to a special place? Could it be a living version of heaven? I felt I would certainly be in heaven never wanting to return to earth? Views of the grey roof tiles that snaked their way upwards blending into the heavy sitting clouds that block out any winter's light, your escape routes definitely shut for at least another day. Winter's grip bringing a silent shiver to your bones as you spent more time studying the zig zag crack on your bedroom ceiling. Had it always been there? Had it got bigger? Was the building going to fall down? Perhaps it was just that you were noticing things now that used to pass you by in your rush to be somewhere else. You looked more for the reason for this the reason for that. The family get together still played out in my mind, mum and dad with their old style dancing, their bodies communicating in the custom of their times. The new pop songs, up beat, allowing the body to wiggle about without the rhythmic, footwork routines of yesteryear. My latest Beatle purchase No 1 again, its simple lyrics, on repeat, work their way to the front of your brain never to be forgotten. "She loves you and you know that can't be bad." It was like a self torture session to lay there with this clear vision of the woman you had fallen head over heels in love with but I needed to play my record, that record over and over. The wait hanging in the air dragging out the seconds as your mind wanders allowing the deep planted seed to grow. Only to pass her house one more time, I must try again. The brainwash of the modern music lyrics play their part in influencing the young minds, should we break out, grow our hair? smoke pot? Not stride for that important job in London Town that commits you to spending your life going to and coming back from work. The time spent waiting for the train is it on time does it drive you to addiction, sucking on the fag, adding an extra pint to the must be in "The Dog and Duck" again this Friday night. That injection of nicotine that floats the brain and prevents the question being asked and certainly never answered. The ticking clock still in no hurry to end the Xmas break as my thoughts bumped off the four walls that held me imprisoned. I spent the rainy time working on my homework, rewriting many times to get my spellings right and that continued demand for deeper expression. The red ink spider may have more trouble this time finding its way to dominate my efforts to impress. I had worked hard at searching my brain for important things to say looking for those descriptive words to beef up the story. Those rides along my faithful routine tracks had allowed my brain to wander, my body needing no mental guidance, cruise control was working overtime.

There were many down roads from my cycle routes that lead back to the Upper Richmond Road. You just sat on your bike gathering speed, no need to peddle as the breeze passed over your ears creating a humming sound. You could zigzag down as well changing routes but that focus remained to end up passing No 10. It was a Sunday so the traffic was light, easy to cut across the Upper Richmond road behind the big red buses that offer a very good service into Richmond or Putney. For some reason I'm not sure why I drew my bike to a halt my hand staying grasped to the brake handle. I had just entered her road I had not stopped all morning but here I was with a must be now feeling running through my body. I noticed my front tyre, a returning habit it seemed of bumping against the kerb. It held my gaze, a moment to collect myself, perhaps I had not wanted to pass without being successful finally in my quest to see her again. The winter break had been long dragging out its ticking hours on a young man's restless brain. A line of cars all parked sheltered my viewing potential. Was her car there? Had she returned? It was back to school day tomorrow. The never ending Christmas break had ran its course my school bag waiting in my room with its assortment of a young man's efforts laid out for inspection. A nervous feeling began to creep through my body adding more attention and perhaps reason for my bumping tyre. She must be there now, could I catch a glimpse. Would she see me? The next move was needed, the line was drawn in the sand, the thou shall not pass tape had to be cut. The brake handle slid from my grip. It sent a signal, time to move on, the next big step of my life had arrived. My bike led the way I had pushed it forward, the line crossed, the tape cut. A slow walk as I straightened my back and stretched my neck. My heart pumping like the time you step on to the pitch to do your stuff, make the pass, score that goal, make your mark.

      I passed a couple of cars as a cooling breeze whistled around my ears. My senses were buzzing, my eyes still searching, the distance shrinking. A clinking of my bike chain accompanied every measured step. Her car was there its sighting sent a flash of tingling through my body. It was like a new being had entered me as I seemed to float over the next few yards. My fingers without command squeezed on the bike handle halting my progress. I was breathing deep like I had ran up a hill at an uncontrolled pace. I needed a moment to gather myself as my fingers remained firm on the brake handle. Only my eyes flitted about confirming yet again that the car was there as another shake, I thought a more controlled shake ran through me. It had been a long wait, time had played about with me enjoying its freedom to bring up and dissect a young man's wandering. Had I affected her the same way, was her mind also taken over my a deep longing to process. She surely had other things to think about, her young child in first place a career but what was next. Could it be me? Would she even want to get involved again? Man these thoughts had played about with my troubled mind. I was possessed, I had followed her car, I had found her house, spied on her, hidden in shady corners hoping to get a glimpse. This surely was not normal, not normal at all.

    Another stiff breeze passed over my ears it's persistent chill aiding my return to the present. I was stuck, out in the open, I needed to move, to get closer, to see if the curtains had opened. I moved forward my fingers still reluctant to loosen their grip but the mind hopefully rules the body. Their sticky resistance faded as I moved towards those light blue doors, the number 10 now occupying my focus. The curtains were open, a soft late sunlight illuminated the room, her son was there playing with an array of toys scattered on the floor. A confusion hit me I was spying again, exposed, out in the open what to do as my eyes checked for observant neighbours. A heat rush was beginning down my spine as the door clicked open and there she stood. I was caught, out in the open with no place to hide.

    I think a few moments passed, my mind went into a swirl all I could do was look at her as those shiny brown eyes looked straight back at me.

"Hello Ross, nice to see you," a little pause followed then she added, " thanks for the Christmas card."

"Oh yes," muttered from my lips, as she walked to her car, my eyes without command locked on her body. The unanswered question hung in the air " How did I know where she lived?" She was dressed in tight jeans, trainers and a thick woolly top tight around her neck. Her hair again short, a recent cut I thought ready for the spring term back to school. She reached in her car and pulled out two bags full to the brim.

"Can I help you with those" I offered placing my bike against the garden wall and needing to gather myself back from wonderland.

" No that's OK, it's just clothes, not heavy."

" Did you have a good Christmas" followed surprisingly quickly from my lips as my mind was absorbed with her sexual allure. Eve turned holding a bag in each hand, her eyes slowly moving up to finally meet my locked gaze. I could feel a moment there, a decision, another positive step needed to be taken. There was nothing I could do, my eyes filled with questions holding her gaze, waiting.

" Come in for a cup of tea," It was like the words were bouncing around in my head had she really said that or was I dreaming.

I found myself back on the railway bridge, another fast train to Waterloo had just done its trick, it's cold rising blast of air scattering my hair in all directions. It focused my runaway thoughts which still needed to be placed in their correct assessment boxes. Was I getting ahead of myself? Was she just being a friendly teacher interested in just another student working hard to pass his summer exams? Was I just another student to her? Would she invite other students into her house as well? There was something about her look, her eyes I thought transmitted a need to connect. I felt I had affected her as well, there was a confidence in me. I felt stronger, a tingle in my body still remained she had definitely taken me over. An invisible injection that floods your body, stronger now more thoughts in the mind and power in my legs to reach the top of the hill, such a short time to feel so different. My hands wrapped around the cold hand rail. My fingers squeezing turning white as the stubborn rail radiates out its own clear message, it's getting cold. The sun now well hidden on its descent, the last light of the day struggling against the grey wintery clouds. It was back to school time tomorrow, definitely getting colder, but I did not want to leave my bridge yet things were not sorted in my brain.

"A cup of tea" she had said it. "Come in for a cup of tea." it replayed itself, at first I was stumped but my head nodded. I had busied myself stowing my bike in the front garden, was this really happening? The wait had been so long, my nerves working overtime to control the excitement that ran through me. I followed her inside still unable to assist as the two bags held her arms tight at her sides. There was a lightness in her movements her body seemed to flow to the challenge or perhaps it was just that my eyes were locked on their target, on my desire. We passed the front room door where her son John was playing with his new Christmas toys and entered the back room. Eve placed the bags in a corner and passed me into a small side kitchen leaving her soft scented fragrance to tickle my nose. I stayed in the back room as there was no room for two in the compact kitchen. The floor was covered by a new matted carpet and the walls were white. There was nothing else, the room was empty, no chairs, no table, no pictures just a small gas fire. Two narrow glass doors showed a compact back garden where the grass was in serious need of a good hair cut. It didn't seem long that Eve appeared with a mug in each hand and handed me one. Her fingers tight around her mug seemed so light and delicate, again her white nail polish doing a perfect job. I felt awkward a bit out of place, having trouble, finding something else to look at other than this beauty that stood before me. Eve leaned back against the wall and slowly slid down to sit on the floor. It seemed such an unusual movement handled perfectly. When there are no chairs I guess it becomes a practiced to perfection event. Her focus held by the garden doors as her mug twisted around between her fingers. Her legs had straightened and her trainers now tapped together, the branded label excellently placed for maximum effect. What was she thinking she seemed so far away at that moment, small and alone sitting there on the floor. Was it letting the past go, trying to move on, things not working out so well. A house to get furnished and sorted, a son to care for and now me standing here with a prominent question mark bouncing off the four walls. What was happening now hardly a situation that gets any votes in the how to behave properly department. I followed her lead careful not to get too close just what one would call a small gap between us. My execution not so smooth not a practice event in my house, sliding down walls. So there we sat tea in hand, many thoughts for sure tracking through our minds. The silence nice in its way but needing breaking the right words lost, somehow hard to find. Perhaps you don't want the end, the words stay hidden. Certain times in your life there's a cocoon that holds you. It's like you reach a point where the moment can't get any better. The body tingles, there's nowhere else to be but right here right now. I had placed my free hand flat on the carpet between us, pressing down to adjust my back a little better against the wall. I'm not sure that it was needed, just a fidget to fill the silence or was the presence of my hand placed there signalling a challenge. A sip of the tea as a follow up then all was still again. Eve had not moved only her trainers now still looking small and delicate pointed to the ceiling. Her hand then moved up to stroke her short hair it remained there active, perhaps on an itch that wouldn't go. It finally came down to rest on the carpet between us a little aside from mine. The space between our fingers so small yet so large, a few inches, nothing at all. Had the challenge been met? Two hands on the floor, two lives at a crossroads. Could those inches be conquered? Such a small gap my hand wanting to move to touch her finger my brain not able to give such a positive command. The ends of her fingers turning white as they pressed down on the matted carpet. Eve's eyes were fixed on the garden doors no movement now of head or arms. The silence was there like another being had entered the room. It had laid down a challenge, reached into the beating heart, the silence helping its presence to grow adding heaps more to a young man's assessment pot.

" Perhaps you should go now," she said, " I have to get organised for tomorrow."

"Yes , of course." fell out of my mouth as her hand retreated silently but swiftly away from mine. A spell had been broken, it had travelled a distance, covered new ground but it still had not reached its final destination. I was polite on my departure offering help if she needed. I was standing bike in hand reluctant to leave as she stood by her light blue door, her hand raised, a silent wave to signal my departure. She returned inside, the door firmly shut the number 10 now holding my gaze. I noticed my breath, my breathing heavy making round circles before the breeze took it away. Time to reassess, definitely progress made she had me hook line and sinker. Those few inches to cross remained imprinted in my mind, our fingers so close upon the floor. I felt disappointment that the touch had not been made to seal our attraction in bodily contact. Time to go home, time to linger on my bridge, to replay every move.

The assessment was done, logged away in a young man's brain. My hands now really numb in feeling finally left the cold hand rail. The passing trains had helped, their motion and gusts of warm air had continued to play tricks on my hanging strands of hair. My bike bounced down the last few steps then across the road. The ice cream signs at Bob's Store's not looking so inviting. Time to be home getting ready for school not sucking on an ice cream. A new year had started where will it take me. I was fit getting stronger by the day, my never ending goal to be a footballer still remained with its own challenge to succeed but now something else. Quite how to put it I'm not sure. The idea roamed around in circles, the way to express it in words, to give it true meaning puzzled my brain. It was something else, something magical, something worth living for. It gave purpose to my peddling every push to get home, to get organised, tomorrow for sure I would be ready.

   First week at school had passed without making sense that there was still twenty four hours in a day. I seemed to operate at a faster pace the effort to do so remaining well within my range. The Thursday night training at Crystal Palace had highlighted my different mood. A cold rainy night had moved us inside to the weights and exercises area under the main stand. Such a different array of potential talent stood at their assigned positions. Me, long and slim with a clear height advantage. Others shorter, more muscular, all with their own ingredients to put into the " I want to be a professional footballer pot," The course set out to test every muscle, exercises to jump and squat, weights to push and lift. The whistle that rings out its command, its squeal echoing in the void setting the confined space into a frenzy of movement. It leaves its echo in your brain as you pass on to the next exercise, to jump and squat, press ups, sit ups. Robby, my games master is not here but I think of him. His territory, strong man, army man knowing the value of exercise to keep the body fit, can you go again without that sharp end of his stick. Ernie our trainer walks around us his body always a clear message of hard work and dedication. His whistle of command swinging around his thick muscular neck as his eye contact demands total commitment to the task. Not a muscle on your body left untested as you begin to hate the rain that beats above. For any exercise there's a mode to be in, the position of your body, your back straight not bending to the iron rod that only gains more weight if your mind wanders. Concentration of the mind, determination, all relevant demanding your total focus. I can move into that zone, that self zone where you step in tune to the challenge. Like a karma effect only with your body working at maximum. That sweat drop again already set at my eyebrow, it gives me a challenge, occupies my mind. It will fall, the load too great, the demand too high but can it be held a little longer? It's there to test me, no doubt a lifelong challenge like many more that lie in wait for the new kid on the block. The time shoots by, the sweaty clothes left in piles as our bodies spar for position under the limited hot showers. Did you remember your soap or your towel always a few scrounging around their preparation not complete lacking perhaps a vital ingredient. Another challenge, be here next week, a match against our local rivals. The notice pinned up giving instructions, 6pm sharp. A statement made, a testing ground, time to move to the top of the class, selection for the chosen few again setting its challenge. To be offered the contract, to sign the contract, to be one to make his mark. You leave the comfort of the warm changing rooms into the cold night air. Your coat prepared fully buttoned with that comfort scarf tight around the neck. The rain now gone leaving a wet damp air that hangs around the street lights. Winter's challenge already nearing its end, time moving so fast now. For those prepared a chocolate bar already half eaten, its sweet sticky taste already offering sustenance to restore the challenged body reserves. A small group is left by the time you reach Thornton Heath train station, again a divide some go north some go south. By the time you hit Clapham station you are alone so many routes home now to split the group. The evening of high activity and demand has ran its course. A scattering of commuters wait for the Mortlake connection. I am alone, my mind now free to roam, its route known within waiting silently for its appointment to surface. The mind occupied, taken over by this wonder in leather boots, such a challenge for a young man's heart. Those visions of Eve as I lay on my pillow at night. Replaying and replaying like my vinyl records all the moments assessed. If only my fingers could have covered those few inches, to have broken through the barrier, to have touched one of those shiny finger nails. There on the floor right next to me, delicate, feminine, attractive, inviting.

    The train finally arrives, its single light appearing through the hanging mist that holds the cold so close. Your coat trying so hard to rebuff the night's cold air but it has been a while and knows its way to finally shiver your bones. The protection of the train instantly apparent as you fall into the window seat. Plenty of room to stretch your legs as your dull reflection in the window occupies your mind. Immediately she's there again, the permutations back, adding confusion to the thoughts of how to move forward. Had I got it right, such a big step into unknown territory needing to be made. The rhythm of the train helping to focus my thoughts, Eve bouncing around, me trying to reach the top of a steep hill to gather my prize. To wrap my arms around her, hold her ever so close and finally kiss those lovely lips.

To be invited inside was a massive plus but obviously it set off alarm bells. Movements made that you have little control over pushing you to the brink. Something you want hanging in the air, can you reach it, does it play tricks and jump away from your grasping hand. The timing not right, best to wait, caution needed to find the right path. I know I'm not alone she feels it as well, that tingle that sharpens your senses. A path to be found that we can walk down together needing more time to plan its routes. I had played the part, I can't say willingly but made an effort. Not passing her house so much wasn't easy to accomplish. I know she needed more time. The abrupt " I think you should go now." The feeling of being so close yet significant ground still needed to be covered. Not to rush it, as the lyrics say, 'only fools rush in where wise men fear to tread.'

Now slowly into Mortlake station its late but the line of waiting cars still stretches away down Sheen Lane. The need to be somewhere, we are made to move, legs to carry us, arms especially to hold the one we love. The train pulled away, such a weight gathering speed, Richmond was next on its railed track. Mortlake station, cold and lifeless but a sense of being back on home ground, only an evening away but its been a challenging day. My walk fast, back straight, with kit bag firm at my side as Bob's Store looms up. A bright light above his door highlighting his offers, the closed notice holding its own in centre position. My gaze goes to the railway bridge, so many trips over it, a place were I can linger a moment, watch the world go my. It has an attraction for me to be high up so close above those passing trains The planes that fly overhead holding your wonder that such a big heavy thing can stay in the air. All on their final decent to Heathrow Airport, travelling thousands of miles, lines of them backing unseen so high in the dark night air. The bridge so close always beckoning another visit but it's not a night to linger as the feel of more rain to come passes on the air. A short walk now down past St Mary the Virgin church where my Dad put the ring on my mum's finger. It kicks up many thoughts in my mind as I traverse the four flights of stairs heading straight into bed. How we got here such a chance meeting, my existence all down to the fact that my Mum was licking an ice cream cone on Richmond Bridge. My ice cream moment I thought to be standing in goal such a rare occurrence and there she walked. My sorting in assessment boxes had been done, my train journey back to Mortlake helping with its rhythm of noise coming up from the tracks. My last thought was there to remember I did not want Eve in an assessment box I wanted her by my side holding my hand. Her hand with those delicate fingers never to leave mine. Definitely my last thought, the most important one for me as my head hit the pillow.

     A couple of days had already passed by, my body had been surprisingly stiff from the intense workout at Crystal Palace. I had used my bike to ease out my muscles, easy on the warm up then a good steady speed without excess. Of course my travels had a focused direction that number ten burning up my brains its magnetic pull too powerful to resist. My confidence remained high, I had built up a pile of pluses, I was going for the jackpot. My determination to succeed had driven my thoughts into overdrive. To have the chance again to cover those few inches, to touch those shiny delicate finger nails, I felt ready to meet the challenge. Quite how to move forward, to make contact puzzled my brain. Could I just appear again at her front door? There's a new movie in town, could I take you? Fancy a coffee and cake at the corner shop? Is it the same as meeting a friend? Does love change the playing field?

Yes, definitely, love changes everything.

January had nearly passed, a few trips over my bridge to linger there and collect my thoughts and build up reserves. The challenge was raising its head again, the big match at Crystal Palace was tomorrow night. This would be my life from now on if I was going to fulfil my dream and cross that demanding bridge to be a professional footballer. I held a confidence inside, on a football pitch I could read the moves, know the timing, hold my own. My control always good, it needed to be as the centre half was always out to get you, hit where it hurts at any opportunity. You could either kick or be kicked, a whole package of being alive, making your mark was wrapped up in the need to be one of the chosen eleven. Could you make the move that tilts the scales, open up the defence to score the goal. Growing into a man, look them straight in the eye my mother had told me one day not so long ago. I had asked her my question that had recently been troubling me. " Where do I look when the teacher is talking and looks at me?" Such a simple answer really but to have eye contact, to make eye contact, to look them straight back in the eye and have time to read what is there. Such good advice but so simple, do they look back at you, is there a second when a signal is given to confirm a connection. To show that you are listening, paying attention, absorbing the knowledge that they are floating in the air. Wanting to learn, pass exams, get a better job, moulded into a good try hard student for the next stage of being alive. There is of course that barrier that is already set, what level on the scale are you? Are you clever? Do you have an analytical brain ready to change the world? Can being clever help, make the world a better place or will it stay a place for the strongest, the man with the gun that fires a thousand rounds. To destroy the man that sees a better future for his people, to keep them down for self benefit, to plunder other countries assets, minerals, diamonds, silver and gold. To fly thousands of miles to engage in a war were the country's people are divided. To pick a side, to become blood brothers in a quest to annihilate a rising force of opposition to your chosen direction. So many ask anyway " Where exactly is Vietnam." My father, his time in Burma fighting the Japanese with his own stories of combat locked away deep in his memory the key truly lost never to be recalled for analysis or debate. The only one to surface was when he was on night patrol in Japanese territory having to cover himself in dirt and leaves. To lay camouflaged on the ground motionless, silent, scared to death that his short life was about to end. The Japanese passing so close, he surely would have been shot and I and my brothers would not be here. Even here on our own doorstep the need to divide and conquer. You see it in the papers every day a country split, labour, conservative, slogans to catch the eye, vote for me and I'll set you free. What is free? Does it exist? Or are we just needed to cast the vote, put your valuable X in the allotted box for the person who smiles at you, who gains your trust by choosing his words so wisely.

Even in my little world in South West London, the wheels turn, now questions being asked, how old are Sooty and Sweep, have we been playing overaged players from our bundle of one hundred and fifty assorted boys in the whole school. The date for our next school game held up for question. Robby says words coming through, other schools asking questions. "Have we been breaking the rules? Playing overaged school boys? Upsetting the hierarchy not acceptable. Could," Barnes Boys School " be printed on that shiny silver trophy. "Winners 1967-68". Obviously silent waves coming from the places of influence, filtering through the grapevine, their origins lost in common consent of rules broken. Does that make the season void or do higher hands take advantage and scribe their name on our cup. Wait and see Robby says but you know from his look, his reddening face, the catch of his eye that all is not well. So you stand on your bridge pulling on your rail, it's still cold and unwelcoming but that is far from your thoughts. You know they will win, the fixers are good at their game. The shiny cup to go somewhere else, to decorate a wall, to stand with others all shining in a row, building success, radiating out its own signal "What a good, successful school your child attends." So there you have it sorted in its box. So much to learn along your way, right or wrong, governed by the system that keeps you in line and holds you to account. Enough time had passed, my sorting done and filed away, the powers that be will put their foot down and remove our glittering trophy, it's so easy for them sitting in their silk upholstered chairs.

  I had to move on, I was ready for the next step. I will play the game, set a marker, put my name on the must sign him list. My other challenge of the heart I had secretly followed, she is always there sneaking in to my dreams as I lay semi conscious in the early hours. I try to touch her with floating hands but my fingers won't close. Something in the way she moves, a floating, attractive sexual presence not to be denied. She smiles back at me, teasing, playing her game with her captured young man's heart. Her smile is sincere, loving, playful. She drifts away out of reach, her naked body like a floating mist you cannot hold. Those eyes so bright and inviting suggestions of good times to come only a few inches away. Everything you could ever want, a perfect chemistry, if only my fingers could hold her close.

    I wake energised and clear minded ready for the next day in my life, my school things sorted, bag packed, a descriptive story laid out to challenge the red ink spider. I'm early for school, my comfort zone revisited, time to spare. I push my bike past numerous blocks of flats along Mortlake High Street. The passing cars in such a hurry send up their own gusts of cold morning air. I have a feeling of being higher, my senses clear of any lurking dust, eyes seeing, a clear picture of where I stand. The low, morning sun trying hard to penetrate the thin hanging cloud. You have checked the weather, no rain today, already assessing conditions for the challenge that lies in wait this evening under glaring, accessing floodlights. The mind to be set, the school day will pass like many others. Your tried hard score on homework hoping for improvement. Your maturing efforts to see the bigger picture. Will it get teacher recognition? Move me up from C to B one step closer to the magic, elusive A. Will the teacher smile at me, pleased with his work on his own battle field another victory to ease his own restless nights. To add value to his efforts to educate the growing, swarming numbers of nodding heads that invade his classroom daily.

    I had reached White Hart Lane, the itch had arrived to mount my bike, my legs messaging a need to start their work. I sat waiting for the gap to start my biking as a car, her car pulled up next to me.
" Hello Ross " she said. " so glad I caught you, can you help me Saturday" It was like the words didn't register properly " Can I help her ?" I think my head was nodding like a happy dog. "See you 10am, OK". "OK" did leave my lips but I was lost somewhere, those eyes had absorbed me taken me prisoner. My sleeping partner had arrived in real life, she had made the next move, the vital move to set our future. I had been planning it, running sequences, acting out my moves, assessing their worth to make sure I could cover those few inches should they ever arrive again. But to happen like that, so simple in a way, the waiting the planning, just to be standing here. To walk my bike and not ride, to

leave early, to have time, to be standing there, that special moment to arrive. The sliding door had played its hand such a mixture of circumstances to form a straight line. A gap from the cars was there to ride. I pushed hard to gather speed, my excitement high, could I see her again. My still moments in wonderland allowing her to cover more ground. She was gone, taken away, the flow of traffic too fast, everyone chasing the rabbit, places to be, things to be done.

Things to be done indeed as I climbed onto the train at Mortlake Station, my timing good all day keeping ahead of the ticking clock. I would arrive early at Crystal Palace but that was the plan, time passes so much quicker when you are late. Keeping time on your side, to go into your space collect your thoughts to step up prepared for the test. I recall teacher Spenser earlier today, his finger raised beckoning me up to stand in the familiar allotted position next to him as he studied my " Try Hard to do Better " story. He remained still looking at the written words, his eyes not leaving the paper to travel over his attended clan and his right hand dangled down without guided movement. His red ink pen hovering, held between fingers on his left hand, flickering up and down holding my attention. There was a moment there when its red nib end lingered above a certain passage. It could have made its mark I was sure but it was held back, the work improved perhaps not warranting a highlight, a correction of red scribble. He handed it back to me after putting a " B " within a red circle at the bottom. His head turning slightly for eye contact sending its message "Good work, much better," or perhaps a question there, " Did you write this?" My day was going well, further contact with my angel was in the diary, only Friday stood between our arranged meeting time. The comfort of the train offering up thoughts to be assessed, does your life just happen in a mixture of just happening to be here or there at a certain moment. To turn that corner or keep straight? Is there any control or is it just a mixed up, jumbled up set of maybe's. Was tonight the test to set my future, to lay it on the line for nods of approval from those high up in the soft, cushioned seats of the dark stand. I was set for the challenge, my confidence boosted by my dream partner. She had appeared like magic, waved her suggestive wand of command and set a faster beat in my heart. There was not any thought of right or wrong, are we governed by the rules of the day or are they there to be scrutinised, held perhaps to account. Are they only made to keep us all in line, to put the money in the slot, to pay your being alive bill on time. The money to be syphoned away to the big house on the hill with its indoor swimming pool, security cameras and electric sliding doors to keep out the inquisitive eyes of the working class nosey parkers.

I was drawn back to my world as the Clapham Junction signs drifted by my window as the train slowed for the station. Only minutes it seemed from Mortlake but my mind had been wandering like a recharged battery giving out that extra glow. A couple of lads joined me on the final lap up to Thornton Heath they made small talk giggling a lot and pulling weird faces to emphasis their jokes. Perhaps the test that lay ahead was too much for them already their minds had gone into overdrive, nervous anxiety running uncontrolled. They were my age as well but I wondered how they still acted so young easily distracted to another topic of giggles. "Was I like that?" I couldn't remember ever being like that, I wasn't like that. I closed my eyes to shut them out the evening challenge upmost in my mind, getting closer with every passing cold, uninteresting station. Soon to be marching up Whitehorse Lane avoiding all the pavement creases, yet another test to set the mind, its warm up challenge to set the tone, to avoid the small talk, to open a waiting door.

Not so much noise as training nights bouncing off the dressing room walls as the chosen to be tested players in their numbered one to eleven shirts jiggled about before kick off. I remained seated, my usual focus on setting my mind in the right gear running on automatic. My whole day perhaps even the whole week was gauged, mentally processed to arrive at this moment. A good week one could say offering up its bonus this morning as the recall of her car pulling up right next to me. " I need your help, " those magic words, the sparkle in her eyes, perhaps a little sprinkle of mischief hiding in there somewhere or was that just wishful thinking. It was time to greet the challenge, my thoughts to be left in their allotted boxes, time and tide had put me here. It was time, "Show them what you've got boyo."

The heated air in the dressing room left behind as you walk in line through the cold echoey tunnel. The end looming, dressed in your team colours, a selection of young men eager to impress. The stage lights up, set, waiting, there is definitely no where to hide. You cross that line to step into another world, that white line that sets the stage, to become someone else, to become a professional footballer. A small crowd under the main stand clapping our entrance, mainly friends and family but always those dedicated hard core supporters running their observant eyes over any future talent. Eyes always on you, eyes on the touch line, eyes hidden high up in the dark stand. I warm up passing a few balls around as my legs open up covering a good stretch of ground. My studs holding firm ready for the test. It's a good night to perform, to show them what you've got, to put a marker down beside your name, to cross that looming long bridge to become a man, a test indeed to make your mark.

    The whistle blows from the man in black, its command sets the match in progress, twenty two players set free to perform their skills. The ball rules the players all responding to it many twists and deflections. The effort needed to gain control, to set the pattern, co-ordination of movement, playing to the strengths of the team. I move well feeling ready and stimulated as my preparation build up processes pay dividends. My early touches sound as we pressurise our opponents and win a corner from a deflected shot at goal. You feel your body, stronger, alive, the adrenaline rush flooding your veins like a potent drug. It carries you, your brain functioning, tuned in, making those runs to open up opportunities. The centre half marking you or trying to tracks your movements waiting for an opportunity to make his own mark, to leave his signature on your leg. The challenge raises its head, as that feeling of being alive floods the body with an assortment of chemicals each one called upon to add its own, special, potent ingredient. They add to the want of being there the reason for being there, good at something, to lay it on the line, to impress those watchful accessing eyes that you have what it takes. To pile up your asserts in one package and lay them out for inspection. You being there with the shirt on, that valuable shirt, the No 9 on your back not on someone else's back. To give purpose, reason for being alive, to have a skill to stand in line for inspection. To get the thumbs up, to be someone, to live the moment. Things that are all part of life's game wrapped up in ninety minutes of combat. Who should win, what ingredient is required to win the day. Will the moment be recalled many years later, its detail placed down in writing to be assessed by indiscriminate readers. To understand a little more what sport and competition is all about. Being in tune with the ball, that touch of control that dictates the next move, the instant control of the long pass to maximise an advantage, to strike at the heart, to ruin someone's day but make yours. Learning all the time, your skills a gift needing to be perfected, moulded to perfection to show your personality, maximise your place in this world. Are you good with a ball or a pen?

The echo of the whistle of command still in your brain as you enter the dressing room at half time. You know it has gone well but no goals on the score board always leaves question marks floating on the air. We had most of the control but goals can be elusive, hard to find especially against organised defences. Those white posts defended at all costs, the task always to strike the perfect shot, to see its curving rise into the top corner. The keeper beaten as his dive falls short of his personal task to keep a clean sheet. It's the goal in my dreams, returning regularly to play its part in setting the mind. So easy in a dream, so hard to accomplish in the outside, tough, demanding, real world. Your studs still bouncing around as Ernie instructs us to stay focused as the hot sweet tea washes around your mouth.

Tea always there in my life, my mother handing me down tea from an early age much too young to remember when. Just a family thing I guess, something needed that fills the air before moving on to something else, "would you like a cup of tea". Of course the addiction has been planted there somehow. Was it the advert so prominent at high viewing time. Those chimpanzees sitting so refined at their table, a cup in hand sipping at the brew. A must watch advert that imprints itself forever in your memory. If that was not enough an added need to collect those treasured picture cards placed so tactfully, only one inside each new tea packet. A few missing cards needed to collect the set, trading with your neighbours, a need planted like putting a "Tiger in your Tank".

My cards still lie waiting in my box of treasures upstairs as I place these chosen words of remembrance down on paper. Another long wait again to see the light upon them once more. To be gazed upon with loving memory of those years so long ago. To recall and witness the delight on my grandfathers face as his one missing card drops from the packet to complete his set. Is there nothing that can't be resolved over a nice cup of tea?

The rest is welcomed, collect your thoughts, a few moments away from the prying eyes. A chance to reset the mind. That extra injection of feeling alive, the dressing room atmosphere bouncing off the heads of the pretenders setting its own unwritten demands for the second half. No changes are made to the team as yet another ten minutes half time rest runs its course. Somehow she has entered my thoughts, opened a back door somewhere and manoeuvre her way to stand before me. That cheeky suggestive smile radiates out of her lovely face so clear and defined. I feel I am no longer alone I have someone, someone to talk to, to hold my hand down life's road to help me put things in there right order. My mind is buzzing, she has added her potion to the mix, set my stage higher, a new level to perform. It's time to lay my skills on the table. The warm dressing room left behind as that extra cold bite gets you as you re-enter the pitch of challenge. The floodlights dominant now, an extra pull on your shirt sleeves as you wait yet again for the man in black to blow. Its sharp echo rings back down from the cold, looming stands. You are set for the test, your body finely tuned, sixteen years in the making to be exposed under these glaring lights. To be fully charged ahead of the game the chemicals flooding through your brains. Decisions you make, correct and driven to succeed. That extra step ahead of the game, the ball there to be controlled your sweet touch working overtime driving the team forward to create maximum effect. There are those moments, magic moments when those jigsaw pieces of being alive fall into place. You operate at a different level, times in your life when you are swept along by an invisible force. Is it adrenalin only or is it why we live, to get to these times when that final piece of life's jigsaw completes the picture. Being there with the number 9 shirt on your back, not on somebody else's back, building a pathway to walk your own road, to become a man.

I was back on the train that was soon to arrive at Mortlake station that feeling of belonging, connecting, still remained floating around my brain. She had come to me, visited, to stand before me in the dressing room, her smile adding that extra ingredient to the pot. My performance, showing my skills, laying them bare for all the prying eyes to witness. To pass the test, to know you had that level of being aware, to show it, to see the pass, to make that run, to perform under the scrutiny of those prying eyes. My body stronger but the day had been long, my reserves had been tested. Again those waiting cars with their stumped drivers tapping away as the train finally passed Sheen Lane crossing slowing for Mortlake, a cold dark uninviting station. Although a winter's chill hung in the air I needed that moment on my bridge, to push and pull that stubborn hand rail. My scarf tight around my neck adding its warm comfort against the winters night. The cold was there hanging in the air waiting for any opportunity to invade your warmth. You know the score, many visits here to sort the puzzle, only wanting a moment to collect yourself. To be on familiar territory, home ground away from those prying eyes. Access your thoughts, so much going on, to get a blast of that disturbed air as the next train passes so close under your troubled soul. Its vibration travels through your body, down your arms and hands that retain their grip, squeezing once again that stubborn, cold hand rail. The swaying side to side motion of the train holding your gaze before it disappears further down its endless, bending track. A testing time, the challenge of being alive, to try and find your path. To share it with someone else who will hold your hand, connect your thoughts, iron out those bumps in the road, make life's journey that much smoother to travel. So small that gap I could see it again clearly as I looked down at my hands, cold on the rail, my fingers pushed straight for some reason, pointing forward. My mind was back in her house sitting there against her wall a clear picture of her hand still just that little bit away from mine. A magnetic pull hung in the air, to go to her house to stand outside to wish that she would just magically appear, open that light blue door, just so I could see her again. To be taken to that special place when that someone else makes all the difference, to be complete. It was time to close that gap, grasp what was hanging in the air, take it by the horns. I was ready, it was time, ten o'clock Saturday morning it would soon come but now it was definitely time to go home, time to reset my clock.

It had taken me a while to fall asleep some parts of my game that night returning for assessment. Was there a better pass to be made, runs I hadn't seen to open up gaps to get to the under belly. I was stretched out on my back, my body still, mind reliving the game but my eyes where searching. Eyes for some reason restless, trying to find the crack line in the ceiling from faint rays of light entering my window from various forms of street lighting. My body was playing the part, sleep was needed but my mind would not settle." I need your help" crept into my thoughts, surely the reason for my searching eyes. Help, help with what? I had wondered if help was needed or contact for another reason had crossed my mind. Perhaps there were things to move, new put it together yourself furniture, finally perhaps a few chairs to sit on. We were in the Black and Decker world now, the adverts flooding through the brain. The man, head of the house holding up the latest must have forward and reverse hand drill. Everyone with their do it yourself kit box, the perfect Christmas present for the modern day soon to become handyman. Buy it in folded pack, "easy to put together" with clear, clear, instruction manual. Easy to put together can be a little miss leading, if you miss that vital little part things can go severely downhill later. I was good at these things, could understand the layout what to do first so we can all be happy campers later with our new modern slim line put it together yourself furniture spread around the house. I will have a few things ready just in case, an opportunity hopefully to impress. Some time was spent going over scenario's of maybe's whilst my eyes finally filtered out that elusive crack line, it was still there, I had found it, at last setting the switch in my brain, to pass over into the much needed land of sleep.

Friday the 9th February was a funny day, I had spent most of the school day feeling above everyone else. Yes I was tall but there was a floaty touch to it, you weren't operating on normal settings. Slow motion on a slight scale, not being quite in touch with your surroundings. My body had recovered well from its put you through the mill challenges of yesterday. I had covered the testing ground, played well, laid it on the line for all to see. Now it was time to focus, to understand why the heart beats faster, why the body tingles with excitement, the modes of anticipation on what tomorrow will bring. Friday, end of weekday free for two days, get all those must do things sorted so next week run's a little better. Next week always throws up more things, part of being alive like old sayings " Get it done now, clear the decks, more to do soon." But this weekend was going to be different, I felt it had a destiny about it, everything about my life stood in the balance. Would Eve respond if our fingers could cover that small gap to make physical contact. A clear signal of the longing held deep inside that had dominated my thoughts. would she allow it to happen would the hesitation of before still hold the upper ground. I reasoned with myself that her hesitation was losing it's battle she had initiated a get together. My presence on her floor, so close creating a release of chemicals that we have no control over determined to have their way. To have some one to watch your back as you stride towards your chosen path. There of course was as always the weekend story, no less than two pages to be covered by those stimulating words of expression. Should I write about what was happening to me, so much to cover it would surely take more than a couple of pages. Could it be put down in writing to be accessed by teacher, passed on for further judgement my those on higher ground who write the rules. Rules, laws, written in stone definitely not to be broken or even challenged. It would certainly be another chance for the red ink spider to strike but the eye contact challenge always there to hopefully avoid its sting. I had mentally penciled in Sunday to cover homework as Saturday I felt sure would uncover a new path for the next stage in my life.

I found myself hovering on my bridge preparing myself for the final walk down to number ten, a few minutes to spare keeping time on my side. My bike left in the downstairs store along with a bag of tools ready just in case a handy man is needed. The thoughts of standing, nervous for sure on her door step with my motley bag of tools did not convey the correct impression I wished to make. I was washed and shaved a few extra minutes spent looking into the bathroom mirror accessing those recent small changes that move a boy into a man. My eyes bright and blue, my chin less pointed and forehead wider with my reliable mass of fair hair with those freelance strands dangling down the side. It had brought a smile to my face, I was a new person, a strength inside that added to that driving need on this special morning. Of course my limited choice of clothes had lead to my faithful polo neck being again in first position, its last outing still vivid in my mind, I just had to avoid sitting next to a log fire. My hands still firm on that cold iron rail its presence always welcoming that feeling of firmness, stability, something to grip and squeeze as you work out the complexities of your life. The various people who pass you by do they eye me with suspicion, that young man there again pushing on the hand rail. No time it seems for them to take a moment to hold that rail, their bridge of sorting surely lying elsewhere. Time also running shorter as your birthday count runs higher. Those endless freelance days of doing this, of doing that now lost in the demands of the day. The ever present need for money, many things waiting to gobble up that overtime bonus of the Christmas wage packet. No time to spare as the must have demands of the TV adverts sink deeper into your brain. All this could be sorted later on another visit, at another time when my life's destiny was not about to take a serious right turn.

      I was ready, it was time as I skipped down the last of the bridge steps. The thoughts of seeing my beauty again adding an extra spring to my step clearing my wondering mind but I knew inside it couldn't last. Every step I took closer to those light blue doors added its own turn of the key to the tightening of my body. I had felt relaxed on my bridge holding that resistant, cold rail on familiar ground but I was walking a different path now. A path into the unknown, where the mind and body send up their own demanding questions that add extra turns to that key in your back. I was there, nervous, stiff as a rod, lean to the left, lean to the right, the bell silent now after ringing out its clear demand.

Do you know that freeze moment? Have you experienced it? When you just stand, looking not quite able to absorb what stands before you. The radiance of her smile surrounding you, cocooned in her spell, unable to do anything but return your own dazed smile. Her eyes so bright holding me, small traces of delicate makeup refining them to perfection, " Come in , come in," she said, " so good of you to come and help," To come, to come I thought I would have run a thousand miles to knock on your door, for this moment to finally arrive.

    I found myself again in the back room with tea in hand wondering if the sliding down the wall procedure needed to be repeated. Eve had busied herself making tea but then disappeared upstairs again. A quick five minutes to my knowledge could well be tested. It had given me a little time to settle, a few moments to collect myself, to remove the key in my back and gain control. My body had started to relax, I was inside again, no mention yet of the help that was needed. No flat packs of do it yourself to be seen, a good decision to leave my bag of tools behind, my services not required in that department. No sign of her son either, his basket of toys stashed in the corner waiting silently for the return of the creative imaginings of a young boys mind. There was something about being near, close to my desire, like the ground you stand on was firmer. A reason for making plans to share ideas, talk about what's happening, what to do next. What to do next ?

      I was back on the bridge, hands firm on my rail, a grin I'm sure was still planted on my face and a keep sake deep in my pocket. We had driven off to Richmond a quest to find a new record player to liven up the house Eve had said. No mention of chairs or tables, the house surely in need of multiple things but first on her list in these modern times it seemed was the must have a new record player. She said she had heard through the grapevine that I knew about these things, a little perhaps but I did wonder if another reason of intent silently waited. The stereo systems changing with every new year, clarity of sound always guaranteed as the price increases. We had driven through Richmond park, a scenic route on a brightening day. I was feeling more relaxed, Eve asking questions about my family and football giving me time I think, to be more in control. Answers were easy so I added a little extra spice to bring a grin to her face. My comfort increased, a little more set I felt for the challenge ahead by the time we left the park. Richmond always busy especially on a

Saturday, numerous stores providing the latest products to supply its more affluent South West London customers. A record player was important in these changing times but so where other useful things like chairs and tables that had lost their hold and fallen down on the modern what's important list. Her driving was fast and controlled but certainly not one to stay in line as another challenge occurred to be again the car in front. Every chance taken to overtake, that burst of speed, the neat change of gear. That potion that lies deep inside waiting silently to surface and add its demands to push the barriers of modern life one more time. The competitive drive to be in front. Competitive certainly came to mind as another car that was in front now trailed behind. It was a risky manoeuvre I thought but its execution so good as to seem normal procedure for a Saturday morning drive through the park. Lady drivers a new thing to me but Eve could drive me around for evermore. I certainly had settled, my legs relaxed in their limited space, hands not finding an itch to be scratched. Her presence seeming to fill the car with an essence of being in a new world. A world that's there to explore, to understand its ways, communicate, take part, add your share to the cooking pot to make it taste that much better. I could feel I was moving into a new world, taking part in its change to leave the old ways behind. To not only challenge the rules but to set new ones that allow the young to express themselves. Not only grow their hair or paint their face but speak up for their chosen course to unite in a kindred spirit and stand together. It was hard to remove my eyes from their desired goal, the hidden magnetic pull that radiated out of this fireball of knowledge that had captured my heart. Was I breaking the rules? Was Eve breaking the rules? Stepping on egg shells this fine February morning looking for that path to get to firmer ground. Will we be seen together shopping in Richmond, will the chains of communication reach that house on the hill with its solid sliding door. Its phone ringing, a scandal, your attention needed to keep it under wraps. Certainly unacceptable under the controlling rules of so called unacceptable behaviour. Can secrets be kept, hidden in shady corners not allowed to surface. The heart that beats inside, it rules your brain sending out the need to be loved, the need to give love. When it takes you over it becomes an obsession, to hold that hand, to walk life's path with that special person.

    It had not taken long to find the music department clear directions to a popular sales destination. Eve lead the way a little in front giving me more time to believe this was actually happening. Her walk firm, direct with straight back, slightly swinging arms, confidence in her stride. The store was busy causing a hum of activity as multiple heads surveyed the enticing array of goods on display. We walked up and down the rows, many items at low cost but the price soon mounting as the clarity of sound added the higher numbers to the clicking till. I was decisive going for a pricy player a friend of mine had already brought a few weeks before. It was a good seller but the assistant said we would have to wait a few days as the stocks had run out and they needed to keep one on display for further sales. Arrangements were made, a phone call when it could be collected, "Quite soon," the assistant had added on producing the sales ticket. Although the cost was high Eve had an account with the store that you paid a little off each month, another good attraction, a fish definitely on the hook to boost the weekly sales. It had surfaced that its was a present to herself, her birthday had been on the 6th February and she wanted something special " for many reasons," she added to mark another passing year. It certainly put chairs and tables in their place the basic necessities not really a special present to yourself on your birthday. The tea shop was next like mission accomplished let's have a cup of tea. Richmond offers up a few narrow alleys along side the open green with tables and chairs offering rest and recuperation from the daily efforts of spending your money. My father to meet my mother so close to where we were just a couple of side streets along from Richmond Bridge. Your life's road determined by sliding doors or being a goalkeeper in the school play ground. We chose a table in a side passage sheltered away from the gathering wind and sat across from each other. I guess this moment was what the day was all about. To sit and look at each other in a quiet out of the way place. We made small talk at first, football had been covered in the park so Eve was explaining her route to end up at Barnes Boys school. I listened quietly her delicate hands occupying my focus as she gently waved them about to accompany her many words of expression. She looked nervous, her eyes not seeming to want my persistent gaze but flicking about checking any passer by. Could she see the longing of a young mans heart the one sitting opposite, the one that loved everything about her. The one whose heart quickened with every catch of her shinning brown eyes. The searching wind had found our sheltered spot, its chill testing our staying power. The tea had been drunk the last few crumbs of the coffee biscuit scooped up to be waste not want not customers. Our waitress setting the tab down on the table as both Eve and myself reached to pay its demand. My fingers falling on hers pressing a little to hold the tab in place. Was it to pay I wondered or to touch their goal? It had happened, like a spontaneous movement, the contact, neither of us moving. No movement of her fingers as her eyes now still looking into mine not flickering off in need or want of a distraction. This was what today was all about to go that extra mile, too accept what was hanging in the air. My desires want to pay the tab had facilitated our connection, traversed an unseen barrier that small gap that seemed so big at first but now concurred. My heart was racing, my polo neck tight but keeping the bite from the encircling wind at bay. She moved a finger to place it on top of mine, softly rubbing in a circle against mine. Its touch so fine, her finger so delicate like a magic instrument of unseen, unknown power to place you under her spell. I already was under her spell, I wanted it not to end, her touch, her touch like a soft, sensitive, electric shock passing through your body to reach the beating heart. I had fallen into her eyes there was no other place to be. I had been accepted, her barriers defeated by the physical demands of the heart. My longing for her proving the same as hers for me. I'm not sure how long we were there, time had no importance but I had managed to pay the tab, smiles and persuasion had won the trophy, that small piece of paper which now sat deep in my pocket. A collectors item, a tea for two price ticket sitting near Richmond green to be placed in my keep box to accompany my other treasures of tea cards and primary school, sports day winners medals for years to come.

Other decisions also had filtered down through the grapevine a senior school football team winners medal would not be finding its way to join my other treasures. The rule makers had made their unquestionable, unchallengeable final decision, rules had been broken, standards must be kept to establish credibility. Our school, my school a little way down Lonsdale Road was not to be presented that shiny cup with Barnes Boys School inscribed on its polished silver coat. No prominent position in the main hall now needed to be found for our cup of shiny success was taking a ride to the school on the hill, no doubt its position in the trophy cabinet already reserved. To have formed such a strong bond, united in our efforts, our assorted group playing above themselves to accomplish success. "Are any of us above that qualifying age of acceptance?" None that I knew of. It was like taking a sickly spoonful of medicine, its sour taste inhabiting, taking residence in the back of your throat. All kinds of lessons to be learnt, some with a stinging taste in your mouth, most I hope without.

    I still had that smile on my face holding my cold iron rail our return home not so rushed. The demands to be in front had lost their morning grip as we cruised casually around the whole park. Using our remaining time together to cover assorted family history in a more relaxed manner. That sitting looking straight at each other over tea for two had covered new ground set a physical connection not to be denied. My eyes now could take a moment away from their goal to enjoy the offerings of a little bit of nature on our doorstep exactly what Richmond Park offers. Time slows as you pass those big iron gates, another world opens up its attractions to be enjoyed by all who enter. A feeling of time slowing down, a relaxed mode spreads as your mind clears. Space to enjoy the green pastures and impressive trees rising on the hills. The pleasing sight enhanced by groups of reindeer scattered underneath, resting close together in family groups. To suddenly find room to breathe not pressed in by rows of houses and parked cars. To escape from the Upper Richmond Road that carries so much noise and congestion. To think more clearly, the calm allowing the mind to process its thoughts. Certainly a place to be treasured. Its pastures waiting to be enjoyed and Pen Ponds a lake to gaze upon with its assorted variety of water birds.   Eve had finally dropped me at Sheen Gate so I could walk home, her free time had run short, the time to pick up her son had arrived. I did not want to leave my seat, to leave Eve, to be alone again. To talk so freely, express your deep thoughts without fear of ridicule to grab the moment to bounce your questions off the wall and receive valuable explanatory answers even on the reasons to fly to the other side of the world. To drop state of the art scatter bombs that destroy without conscience the sporadic villages of wooden huts that sit on open farmland. To kill indiscriminately the local Vietnamese farmers along with their wives and children who have only rag clothes on their backs. My mind was bussing like a new door had been opened revealing a hidden array of questions to be answered. Eve responded with measured replies accompanied by extra hand movements to cover sticky ground. My eyes always attracted to her delicate fingers as they waved about adding weight and heightened   emphasise to her decisive viewpoints. Sometimes there where clear reasons if you accepted a certain view point but most positives had hidden negatives to add extra angles to the debate. Conversations like this I did not know, many thoughts like this had traveled through my mind without outside added assessment of the root cause of decisive actions. It was time to leave the outside world behind, people are paid well to sit in selected, guarded rooms. To come up with acceptable, agreeable ways to move forward, many ways to manipulate a tangled mess but always avoiding it seems placing their finger on the button once again.

So intense were the topics under debate at the end that another meeting or see you again soon had not been arranged. A quick I must go from Eve as she realised the park had absorbed us, time had moved on and her attendance was in demand elsewhere. A longing for more, another time to meet or go together to collect the new record player, the chance had been missed causing my gripping hands to pull hard on that tough, resistant rail. My left hand then unknowingly rummaging in my pocket bringing out that small tab of tea for two. My mind again taken over picturing her finger rubbing softly over mine that feeling of injection again that sparks the body and rules the mind. This was my place, to stand here high up on my sturdy bridge, my assessment complete. The warm touch of my desire still holds firm ground in my imagination as the tab yet again draws my attention. A new, strong love floating on the air needing to be caught, definitely not going to be denied. The devious ways of the outside world I happily leave to those selected few smartly suited officials, but will their next decision be wise for all mankind or only benefit the hidden rule makers lurking in the shadows

  There's a moment before waking when your eyes are seeing but not able to open. Light flashes seem to move around X raying tiny veins in the thin skin, but your eyelids remain shut. Sunday had arrived a little late as my conscience registered the morning sun beaming through my bedroom window. I remained still happy with my eyes reluctance to open, the covers tight and warm a few minutes perhaps to recall a special day. It had been hard to fall asleep the night before so many things warranting further reflection. So much had happened, such progress made, the question always surfacing could I have made more impact, presented myself in a better light. Not rambled on with a sixteen year old's review of world events but then I was sixteen and the world seemed a little more towards accepting the views of the young. It had seemed so natural sitting there beside her as we drove pass the many impressive trees of Richmond Park. Their bare branches waiting silently for the warmth of spring to cover them again in wide lush green leaves. Being in the park on familiar ground had helped me settle. My questions on why this and why that had taken up a lot of our time. Topics that had been left on my back burner suddenly out there for debate. Interesting to receive such full detailed answers, there was certainly clever ways to present the plusses and minuses and Eve was without doubt a master at that, certainly in my eyes. Not always a definite this or a definitely that, just to talk, to lay it on the table and serve it up piece by piece. Plans needed to be made, to be ready, for I was certain Eve had fallen in love with me as well. To be here with her, to have made a reason, excuse even for needing my help. There had been a presence of connection in her car, two people talking, taking their time, new moves required to arrive together as one, our bodies ruling the day, care needed to walk the next passage in our lives together.

  I had worked my way out of my frustration mode into positive territory. My eyes sticky resistance to opening had finally ended, the sun already high carried no warmth. My body rested, still cocooned in covers but it was time to move. Get yourself up, be ready as I felt sure the next stage was about to present itself this driving force that had invaded my body would not leave unrewarded.

Sunday seemed a long day my late arrival not helping to quicken the clock. I made use of the clear skies my bike welcoming its exit from the store shed to cover again those familiar routes. In such a short time so much ground can be covered, the freedom to explore although my territory was like a clear map imprinted in my mind. Up high in Richmond Park, the tall buildings of London protruding into the sky soon another one to be the leader reaching new heights. Your eyes following those noisy planes as they glide down over the city to land with such perfection on those slim runways thousands of miles apart. The thought that only yesterday the park had been the place to be its attraction clear, the open spaces, a moment of calm, a place perhaps to fall truly in love. A little like a drive to the country assures an escape, a breathing space from the confinements of the crowded streets of outer London. I had made use of a well placed seat to watch the planes, take a moment, its not usual for me to stop but my bike was still. I had made a decision, decided to buy the Beatles album Sergeant Peppers Lonely Hearts Club Band. It had been out a while, a best seller, a must have attraction for the young but albums were expensive and my weekly pocket money had many other avenues to disappear. I had a little in my keep box it would be my first album purchase its lyrical tunes already embedded deep in the mind. Of course there was the hidden reason, not hidden really just trying to think of the next way to move forward. The new record player, a present for her shaping my thoughts, something to give her. If I could arrive at No 10 holding it forward, my birthday present to her, the fab four to sing their songs to us. To slide that shiny, black vinyl record out of its white sleeve, place it with care in position for that needle to work its magic and fill the room with The Beatles. Something attractive even puzzling about the spinning record holding your gaze, how is that tiny needle able to reproduce such a clear sound. Of course I was getting a little ahead of myself but my mind was spinning in all directions. There was a need to be with her, close, absorbing the confidence that radiated from her. To share again that touch, that presence, with its mixed ingredients that takes first place, the perfect cake to eat. A passing wind had ruffled my hair another day loosing its grip as the sun began to sink yet again ticking another day in the life. Time still needed to fill those two waiting blank pages in my homework

box. What could I write about? Was it possible to lay out a young man's heart for assessment, to take a risk that all would be well, to produce the right words of expression that can be acceptable in these times of change. Would you really expose yourself to the rule makers for serious assessment. For them to have something new to chew on, to dig deep. Their minds active, alert searching for those expressive words used so carefully to denounce such unacceptable behaviour. No rocking of the boat to be allowed under their rule. Did they never venture away from the straight line? Where their school days never tested to take a side turn where body rules the mind. Are rule makers free of any hidden deeds from younger years that if surfaced could lead to dismissal of rank. It definitely was not for me to resolve, my next job waiting to once more avoid that hovering red ink spider. A plan was laid out in my mind no need to spend more time on my bridge of decisions, straight home to be fully prepared for tomorrow. My bike waiting to do its job yet again taking me home, its route programmed to perfection
just like those massive planes overhead pinpointing that slim runway for landing at Heathrow Airport

      Monday had not only arrive but set many more bouncing balls to be controlled, plans definitely had been made. School had passed in a flurry of moving from one classroom to another. There was always the final lesson of the day waiting like a mountain to climb. My two pages of must be at least two had turned into four, well nearly four. I knew some spelling was wanting further attention but my mind had chosen to make a challenge, like a statement, write it out as it comes not slowing the pen to correct this and that. The flow of writing had taken me by surprise, the words spreading out offering context and expression. I knew the red ink spider may have a field day but somehow the importance of crossing all the t's and dotting all the i's had lost its grip on my need to impress and gain acceptance. Checking over my hastened work showed a new view point, I knew it was good, the longer words of expression adding not only weight but emphasis, more expression. I could look forward with confidence to that eye contact and smile at that red ink spider should he feel the need to shed his ink once more. Perfection can be found in many forms its need for tidy and polished presentation only important if you have a mind to make it so.

    The whistle of the wind accompanied me as my sturdy bike made steady ground carrying me back to Richmond. I had taken a few moments waiting outside the school gates the wanting to see her again stopping a quick escape to fulfil my plans. The need to look everywhere, to be observant just in case, only to see her again one more time, hoping, wishing to get the next contact sorted, to have it in place to meet again. Its not a long ride to Richmond but my ears were certainly turning white by the time I entered the record shop. The warn air gust fanning out from a machine above the door adding a comfort for the spending customers. An array of posters covering the wall, super hit stars of the day peering down on you as you sift through their latest vinyl LP's racked out attractively for your inspection. It was easy to find, your chosen gift, to place your hand lightly on that cover of multiple attractions, this record to be my birthday gift to Eve, those four famous suited lads from Liverpool staring back at me as I open the forded cover. Of course you are tempted to linger, to stay warm, to filter through some more racks, your fingers active flipping over the shiny covers but the prices always causing hesitation, stretching the limits certainly of my piggy bank. My plan for the day running its course, my birthday gift to Eve now carefully placed in my school bag. My school books gone all left in the store room at home, not one accidental mark was allowed to tarnish my first vinyl LP album. The return home even colder as your bike lights flare out, concentration needed in the compact rush hour traffic. You mount the four flights of stairs to reach the top floor. You don't consider them a challenge they are just there, a part of life, the access route to your front door, your home. Mum sometimes leaving the heavy shopping in the store room waiting for my brother or me to arrive home and do the carrying for her. The record now safely home laying on my bed pillow occupies my mind. I study the cover, read the song titles, slip the record out a little bit too gaze at the shiny groves across the black vinyl. The record slides easily back into its white compact sheath of protection. Its magic sound tucked away, waiting, its presence keeping me company, waiting for its moment to arrive.

      The evening passed with many wonderings of the mind. My school books back in their bag tidied away for another day. The red ink spider had enjoyed his day spreading out his many corrections but I had received another B encircled at the bottom with " A little more care needed " written underneath. Yes, I should have tidied my work a little more but sometimes it's good to just be a normal sixteen year old and just kick the system now and again. I was restless, visions of Eve floated around, my longing growing to have the magic of her touch, the attraction of those inviting lips sending its strong message to my heart once more. I had spent more time lingering in my bedroom, eyes needing regular checks to make sure the record was still there, like it was not real or could suddenly disappear in a puff of smoke. Its assistance needed, that magic sound to be present, filling the room with its modern rhythms as my hearts wish to kiss those shiny attractive lips would finally present itself.

A letter had arrived as well, my mother presenting it to me with some amusement as letters for me were virtually non existent even at Christmas time. I had examined the letter before opening, just I think to make the experience last a little longer. Were there any clues to its origin? The post mark smudged above the stamp but definitely posted in London. I had opened it with care using a peeling knife from the kitchen, my mother hovering close obviously sharing my interest. The single forded paper inside now opened showing a prominent Crystal Palace logo as my eyes scanned down the typed words. I had made the grade, passed the test, reached the standard required to be an apprentice professional footballer. My Mum asking, her need to know breaking the spell a little bit as my eyes remained fixed on the tidy typed words. My efforts to impress had succeeded that last match against local rivals sealing my future, confirming the confidence that traveled through my body was not mine alone. My mother planting a kiss of congratulations on my cheek the offer of a contract of employment still holding my attention. School days soon to be finished, a line drawn, exams in June then sign up and present yourself prepared and ready for your dream to come true. Things falling into place a line of events working their own path to make order out of a mixed bag of maybe's. My record player with those magic 45's finishing another day with those four from Liverpool, " She loves you and you know that can't be bad."

      Tuesday had a way of its own to slow the ticking clock, I was fidgety, an unrest had invaded my mind. The lack of known contact again had troubled my sleeping hours which had led to passing through the morning without consciously being resident in my school chair. Being with her on Saturday, that time together alone, those magnetic eyes, to read what lay there, their glowing, magnetic attraction unavoidable. The soft touch of her finger its unseen ability to file away everything else into the totally unimportant box. The afternoon finally spent on Robby's makeshift assault course a good place for me to be at last. A way to land back on solid ground to get your act back together. My body enjoying the challenge, I stay focused, the weights cold and heavy but controlled. I'm back in the zone I know, on solid familiar ground, my body heat rising as Robby drifts by lingering a while to make prolonged eye contact perhaps a question lurking there, something hesitant in his stance as our eyes lock in unison, definitely a puzzle to be resolved. Are teachers trained to watch for unfamiliar behaviour, to have a sense of detection like a radar that spins around looking for the eye that turns away showing discomfort, even exposure. Many hidden thoughts not only mine carried in the classrooms of nodding young heads. My sweat drop starts growing, it's path to my eyebrow a short journey but today is a day to hold it there. My concentration grows, the pleasure of the task felt deep inside, your body cruising, I am back in the present whole again, my mind clear certainly ready and waiting for the moment to arrive. The school bell ringing out surprising me that the time has yet again taken away another school day. My weights replaced to the shelf as my hand rises to wipe away that hanging sweat drop, my task accomplished, the usual chaos of escape around us as we tidy away more equipment. I observe the first year students as they scramble passed me looking so young and innocent. To grow up so fast, five years only since you left Sheen Mount Primary School. Does needing to be a professional footballer age you quicker? The demands of physical competition on your body, a defined driving force that takes your brain to a new operating level. Your arms and legs driven to stay in touch with your brains firing demands. Your heart pumping to supply the oxygen that feeds your muscles to be a winner. To get the nod of approval. To make solid eye contact with your peers and understand what is written there. To get approval from your father, observing silently in his favourite shadowed corner.

R o b b i e sitting on a bench calls me over his hand waves with purpose beckoning me to sit with him as the hall finally empties of fleeing youth. I had read it right, definitely something in the air needing to be tidied away, a quiet private word perhaps. Thoughts naturally shift through my brain." Have I been spotted?" Eyes in the walls perhaps but I know I'm on solid ground with Robby. We talk a bit, a means to get to the sticky bit I think as his face starts to redden. That connection between two people a bond between us to work its way to the target. The football cup not coming our way our efforts to succeed highly commendable but the powers that be not up for questioning. He looks sad, a man obviously that likes to meet a challenge face on with the cards on the table and succeed. Not be stabbed in the back by the knife that has no known owner, powers that be have many places to hide. I tell him my news that Crystal Palace want me to sign up, a smile returns to his face as his hand searches in his pocket, this is it registers in my mind. He slips me a sealed envelope, "For Ross" it says could it be from Eve? It must be. He holds my eyes for a moment, searching. Nervous, I break eye contact and look down at the sealed envelope the two words still there holding my gaze. I'm sure his eyes remain on me, do I give the game away, are forces at work to dig deep. I think not, definitely not from Robby as I look back up to again meet his persistent, inquisitive, questioning eye.

    My note read many times, more than my letter from Crystal Palace now only holding second place tucked away in my keep box. Just a few words upon the white paper but read so often its hard to believe I haven't warn the writing out. Come tomorrow at seven, I have collected the record player. Can you bring some records to play? Eve. You could say a kind of magic was shooting around my body like a high energy drink had been consumed that energised by very soul. The way the afternoon had set me back on track, the negatives all laying defeated scattered on the ground around my feet. The next path to her front door had been laid out, a message that had traveled through the school grape vine, a few simple words that now occupied my brain. No need to travel again the long and winding road, my spying on my desire days were definitely over. My Sergeant Pepper's record now carefully wrapped in coloured gift paper to be handed over tomorrow night. Its opening to set the stage, Lucy in the Sky with Diamonds, such magical words to bounce off those four white walls. My dream now sitting in the waiting room, does it have any chance to become real, to become true and offer up the perfect moment at long last to kiss those inviting, promising to arrive in heaven, lips.

    A switch had gone off, the day was done, everything was about tomorrow. No need to linger any more on detail I needed my rest for I felt not only another big day in my life would arrive with the morning light but a day that would govern the passage of the rest of my life. Reset my clock all was in place, my gift ready, sorted boxes, control back to perfect, now it was a time to just let it be.

    I was surprised how well I had slept my mind on recharge not even a casual glance needed the night before to relocate the travelling crack line. I remained still a slow beginning to this day of reckoning. The thoughts of it causing a long stretching for my feet to locate the end of my bed. My arm then searching under the bed a moments fright before it finally located the offerings of a lonely heart. My gift still safe there, hidden, tucked under my bed for safety and also to avoid the sighting of my brothers prying eyes. A few seconds more to linger in my comfort zone, warm and safe but life's road especially today needs walking. A path laid out that my heart demands I walk, no other place to be that sharp pointed sign on the wall that shows the way, a No 10 doorway gazed upon so often in recent weeks. How will it go? Like the end of the perfect movie were the hero gets the girl and all is well for ever after. How often does that really happen, is that why we like it so much rate it so highly No1 best movie of the year. Will I look back on this time of my life many years from now and recall every fine detail of its unfolding. Would that be possible to recall exactly how a young mans sixteen year old beating heart can cry out for love. The driving force that it processes to reach its goal, the ball without doubt to strike its target once again, the top corner of the back of the net. To place it down on paper for the mixed assortment of questioning eyes to form conclusion on its authenticity. That surely would never happen, just puppy love not how things happen in the real world. There's standards and rules to safeguard us against these slight deviations away from the norm. Will your older love later be more secure love then? Surely strong enough to build a partnership for life? Is that how it works like a process on a conveyer belt to be exactly like your next door neighbour. If that's so how come the queues mount at the divorce desk so many people around just like my uncles looking for escape, roads chosen without solid guidance, the cement turning to dust and blown away on cold, wet winters nights. The time spent in the Dog and Duck, drawing on the cash flow, the need to be home not so controlling, not so demanding. The late welcome home not so bright, no candles lit, no dinner in the oven to satisfy another hard working yet again monotonous day at the office.

   The day at school, organised and regimented, running smoothly on its tracks just like so many before but not so for me. Lunch break was dragging out its minutes, my thoughts starting to accelerate I guess as I stood again in goal of first sighting. My head turning with every slow, waiting minute. Would she walk passed again, I would know for sure, feel her presence, be alert but this time surely turning her head to look straight at me. Those promising seductive eyes to work their unseen wisdom, to connect the dots, to send the message again without sound or lip movement, the one clearly imprinted in my brain ," See you at 7."

Do you know about these feelings so deep that have no boundaries, no restrictions that can be laid out to block their path, have you been there, taken over by unseen chemical forces. To be prepared as you walk down your life's road when it turns knowingly a little away from the norm, to take the risk, to know if not taken, you would regret it for the rest of your life.

Yes, school, my school was over its work accomplished for another day in these changing times. How long can it go on I wondered collecting my bike from its sheltered, patchy place behind the school. The tired, red antique brickwork showing many signs of weathering decay its corroding areas repaired many times but not hiding its slipping downhill path. Its roots way down deep in the ground but struggling now to find water in demanding times. It's mixed bag of teachers and pupils, each day absorbing the energy that flows from inside the closed, loosely fitting, classroom doors. Bigger, modern, new schools now offering so called higher standards of education. Sports with those winners silver plated cups and shields for open display, leading the way to becoming the show case of success.

It's funny, the things that enter your brain, trying to make rhyme or reason out of life, your life. Things needing to be left for another day as I skipped my bike into motion, homeward bound, leaving school behind, finally my ticking clock had started to speed up.

Back at home alone my back firm against the wall, I sat on my bed surveying my bedroom, the place of rest in my world. Such a small room really, no wall space left just two single beds against the opposite walls to accommodate my brother and me and a set of draws to hide away our assortment of odd socks and old pants. Our record player covering the only available surface space, frequent trips carrying it into the living room to liven up a cold, long day at home. My brother hardly here anyway the eighteen months difference in age already absorbing him well into the nine to five thirty work force zone. His own escape at weekends to be one of the boys sitting proud and coated on his scooter at Brighton Beach. My kit bag under my bed already sorted away for Thursday night training. To know that you had made the grade, your confidence in yourself gaining recognition from those eyes hidden in the top cushioned seats of the looming stand. All these wondering were about tomorrow and what will be will be. Now what lay at the back of my mind resting had moved forward to occupy clear unchallenged first place. My beauty with those alluring eyes that take your breath away. Her movements all coordinated to flow over the ground with grace and purpose. A sexual, female presence that can't get any better. That letter of connection delivered through safe reliable hands, the words clearly written, the unwritten words waiting silently in the wings.

    Such a change was happening already to become a new person than the one before, to move into a world where everything is linked and reasoned, a world to share, to be together, me to love another and have that hand to hold.

    I had shaved, combed my hair into straighter lines of acceptance in the mirror but knew it would not last. My hair having a mind of its own also to mould the shape it wants. We will live together is the only answer to that puzzle as I glanced around for my worn trainer shoes. It would be nice to have a pair of blue suede shoes to tap together waiting for that door to open. One could dream but all those material things could only reach so far up the love ladder, the tune that played in one's heart was all that mattered The door shut firmly behind me as I scratched an itch under my reliable polo neck, a slight echo of my downward steps on the cold, featureless stairway. The apartment above now empty waiting silently for the next key to turn its lock. Dad surely finishing his day at his allotment preparing so many neat lines of vegetables for the coming spring and Mum collecting younger brother Roger up from the after school minders. It was a little early but I liked early, the sky already darkening but clear of clouds. No place for my bike tonight, left safe in its store as I walked the walk. A few 45s swinging in a hanging bag but that special vinyl record tucked safe, cushioned under my arm. Within no time standing on my bridge, solid home ground, those few extra minutes eaten up massaging that cold hand rail watching those rush hour trains appear and disappear down their railed track. The tingle starting in my neck sending a cool evening shiver down my spine. I knew it was starting, couldn't hold it any more, my control had been good, focus to get me this far to my trusted bridge but now the moment was drawing near, definitely to be on the other side of the tracks. A couple of deep breaths, time to go, walk the walk, enjoy that tingle that invades your body, embrace it, for you definitely want this moment to arrive. The ring of the bell, standing as ready as you can be, your hands occupied holding your birthday gift, nerves kicking in again as the parcelled record begins to shake in your hand.

The wonder of that door opening, the smile that says it all taking you to another place in time. To be transported into a different land as her hand with those so delicate fingers reached out to receive the offering of my lonely heart. Her fingers resting on mine transmitting their signal, my eyes on those shinny white finger nails as my squeaky happy birthday words left my mouth. I followed her into the back room giving me a chance to remove the waiting tear drops from my eyes, my emotional level running on overdrive. The new record player stationed there on the floor still in its box of moulded foam. A new side light with coloured glass placed in the corner offering soft atmosphere away from the central ceiling light. My hands busy removing the taped wrappings as Eve made tea for two. A time to settle a bit, if that was possible, breathe deep I thought just like recovery from Robby's exercise course. Something to do thank goodness, take your time, unwrap the box. Eve returning with the tea her expertise in sliding down walls showing again as no tea was spilt. She sat still against the wall watching me with shiny mischievous eyes, a letter suddenly appearing in her hand placed on the floor, it drew my attention 'For Ross'. What was it?

The new player finally lifted from its wrappings to be set down on the matted carpet.

My bag of 45's already spread upon the floor ready for assessment. The plug entering the socket not perhaps a space trip to mars but I had certainly taken off into another world. If I wasn't already in heaven I was certainly knocking on heavens door. The need to gaze upon her, every movement no matter how small attracting my eye. My hair playing it's part of discontent fulling across my eye line but keeping it in order tonight was not on the priority list. My gift leaning against the wall next to Eve still unopened but offering a pathway, a connection.

      The magic box now playing with an assortment of 45's, the words clear filling the room, covered in meaningful expressions of the times. Let's go to San Francisco with flowers in her hair, she loves you, I want to hold your hand. There were many of course coming at you every week, their meanings clear but words sometimes massaged to cover hidden lifestyles of changing ways. Pop stars under investigation for use of illegal substances but how can you write about it if you have not experienced it?

      My back now against the wall with foot tapping to the beat. My wrapped present of entry between us and that tea in left hand to offer assistance. My right hand placed in the gap between us waiting for connection as my little finger scratched on the matted carpet like a worm on a hook, perhaps hoping subconsciously to attract her eye. I was calmer now so close to Eve, settling you could say, the music, setting the tone, certainly helping to cover my nervous anticipation. Eve's hand coming, her little finger softly touching the record cover before finally resting on top of mine. It was a warm touch, resting there, carrying its message straight to my heart. Was it time, had it arrived that need to kiss those lips, its presence mounting, a growing need, should I make the move, was it now or never. Her hand moving from mine too quickly I thought to gather the present, a little more time needed. The rustle of the wrapping paper as it slid off my gift from the heart. The shiny cover of modern times needing close examination, a moment of calm as I still felt her touch upon my hand. " You must put it on to play," she said, springing up so suddenly to enter the kitchen. I reset the player to 33's, a time to gaze upon that shiny black record as it left the cover, its promise waiting there, times were changing, my life's road was certainly changing. Eve reappearing, a plate of sandwiches placed between us as Sergeant Pepper set the scene. The sound so clear, most of the words already known so well, joining us to travel our new, adventurous road together.

With 'a little help from my friends' it had happened, that undeniable force that rules the body had won the prize. Lucy in the Sky with Diamonds with that must sing along together chorus had opened the door. The song just starting, its lyrics already planted in the brain as Eve offered up the white folded letter waiting with occasional, inquisitive eye contact so patiently on the floor. Its seal not licked as the card slipped easily from its cover. Many hearts of colour greeted my eyes, the words clear and punchy, " Would you be my Valentine tonight? Eve " I did not know, February the 14th taken up with so much, but not a time for more wonderings as those eyes finally, without hesitation reeled in their prize. My lips now on hers, the kiss, it's magic flooding every vein in my body. My hands around her feeling her need, her desire so strong adding that extra potion to finally take you away and place you on the road to heavens door. The rhythmic vibrating sounds of the times now losing their grip, only a background noise now in the place we had entered. A place, our place, sealed off from prying eyes as we laid together on that matted floor, the perfect place to be. Kissing those lips with such welcoming assistance, the discovery of yet another world, a new land to enter, the land not only of loving but being loved in return.

The need to remove my tightening polo neck, not wanting to break the spell, not wanting to remove my searching hands from their treasured possession. A need so great for I thought my heart would explode as I held her so tightly. To remove my top without leaving those lips of such hidden, magnetic desire, a challenge but definitely not possible. I knelt above her, polo neck removed bare chested, my hair a shambles as my fingers tried to make order out of chaos. Eve was smiling , her brown eyes shining like a certain weight had been removed from her life sitting up so smoothly to touch my arm. "Come," she said taking my hand, her touch so delicate like holding a prized procession, never wanting, never ever wanting to let it go. My stairway to heaven, our stairway to heaven together had arrived those few steps to the bedroom at No 10 never to be forgotten. "Wait here," she said as I sat upon the soft mattress in the back bedroom. Did I notice much I'm not sure, my heart needing more of the potion, wanting to pump again at top speed. To remove all my clothes to lay there, the anticipation building was there a crack in the ceiling? To follow its route, to pass a little more time to control a runaway heart. No curtains covered the two big windows allowing some rays of moonlight to enter. A plane heading for Heathrow its headlights entering the room casting a few seconds of extra shadows in motion across the room before its noisy passing over head. My eyes back on the ceiling as Eve returned naked to slip so delicately between the sheets. A scented presence, a female fragrance so demanding, her warm, caressing body to lay upon my beating heart. A joining to become one not to be denied only to be witnessed by the lights of those noisy passing planes with their small round windows closed to my world below.

    Eve had slipped away a few minutes she said as my reaching hand lost its hold. To lie flat, to be alone for a few seconds, to know for certain that she would return. Is it possible for someone to take your heart, to hold it in their hands, to have total command over it, for I felt this had happened to me. I could not offer silver, gold or even a house on the hill to live in. My bike tucked away in its store my only real possession but I was living my life, taken that decision to never look back and regret a pathway not taken.

    We talked, many things on the news needing attention for the why this and the why that. To have made that connection, to cross that bridge, for lying beside her was just the perfect place. The uneaten sandwiches retrieved from the room below to be eaten without dropping a crumb. Time had moved on,

Sergeant Pepper to be played many times, its magic moment for sure to be remembered for the rest of my life. My bike rides down long and winding roads had reached their goal, a new route discovered to open up my heart and have a hand to hold as I walk its path.

Wrapped up and ready, time to go home. Eve to walk a little way with me her hand still in mine, her soft tightening fingers squeezing like a morse code message going straight to my heart. "To my bridge," I said as those doors of such promise closed behind us. Her gloved hand still tight in mine, standing there as the first train threw up its chilling gust of night air. I explained my many trips here to sort my puzzles, to get my boxes in order. The questioning people that pass over do they look at me and wonder what I am doing. "Always here when I pass?" "What is he doing?" Pushing and pulling on that cold iron rail again. Their questioning eyes always dropping away as their pace to pass increases. Eve looking up at me, smiling I think at my schoolboy ramblings. "You just tell them that you are Throwing Buns to Elephants. Her hand raised ready, the throw of the imaginary bun to the next passing elephant, to mimic throwing buns to elephants. Throwing Buns to Elephants, did that really happen? Just like that, to come out with such a thought, to put it all in context. Now I would have my answer to those questioning glances on the bridge that blows my hair and rattles my bones. For what business is it of their's anyway. It was my place in my world to stand here to sort my puzzles of life and file away the answers. Their hesitant glances may well remain as they pass me by heading perhaps for their own location for getting their troubled moments into order. For I had entered a new world now, my life's path to walk, it's route unknown but such a delicate hand to hold now as I travel it's path.

  The slow train into Mortlake its driver waving, acknowledging the two people on the bridge waving their arms about laughing. He was not aware his train was covered in buns. Nothing for me to do, the moment so perfect to place my lips so softly on Eve's. The passing fast train heading for Waterloo sending out its own high pitched whistle of approval, its rolling wheels taking it many more miles towards its destination before our goodnight, final, love you forever kiss of the night was over.

Thank your teachers for their efforts to make shape out of muddle. To show a pathway to express all your talents. Would I had ever thought or dare to write a book in my future. To use those pointers shown by my special teachers of Barnes Boys School, a little ways down Lonsdale Road. Their daily efforts to allow the young to live their lives. To not only teach but influence us on the values of honesty, acceptance of wayward issues handled so well when wanderings from the straight and narrow take place. For their guidance not to be rigid and unbendable. I thank them and dedicate this book with my efforts at words of expression to them. I have tried my best to be as accurate as possible and avoid the red ink spider if that will ever be possible for me. I thank you for reading it, such a wonderful experience, my life, to have walked its many miles hand in hand with Eve my wife, our son Ross, my stepson John, and their extended families.

This book was written by an ex-professional football player in 2023. Its last words placed down on new years day 2024.

Printed in Great Britain
by Amazon